Published by Pedigree in association with **Yours**
Pedigree Books Limited, Beech House, Walnut Gardens, Exeter, Devon EX4 4DH

Yours – the read of your life every fortnight!
Look out for it in your local newsagent.
Yours, Bauer London Lifestyle, Media House, Peterborough Business Park, Peterborough PE2 6EA.
Tel: 01733 468000

Compiled and edited by Sharon Reid
Designed by David Reid
Sub-edited by Christine Curtis
Additional writing by Marion Clarke, Michelle Nightingale, Sheena Correa, Jade Pickering,
Laura Bradder and Sheena Harvey

Bird of the Week supplied by Bird Watching, the UK's best-selling bird magazine.
Visit www.birdwatching.co.uk
Selected Bright Tips from How to Squeeze a lemon by Fine Cooking Magazine,
published by Taunton Press, £14.99

**Special thanks once again to the readers who have contributed so wonderfully to this Year Book by
sending in their memories, precious photographs, stories and tips**

◆ All telephone numbers, website details and dates correct at time of going to press

Welcome to A Year with **Yours** 2012. This is our 10th year of producing the **Yours** annual – and every time we sit down to start planning a new one I worry about how to make this year's book even better than the last. I needn't be concerned though because, as usual, **Yours** readers have come up trumps by sending us so many wonderful stories, precious memories and evocative pictures.

We've smiled at your teenage antics and shed a tear or two over your touching 'Our Tune' dedications.

This year we've also included a treat for crafting fans – an easy-to-follow project for every month of the year.

Alongside all this we've managed to pack in 52 tasty recipes, lots of money-saving tips, scores of your precious photos and a range of eccentric events taking place across the UK. We've also got short stories, fun quizzes and a few surprises along the way.

With your help I'm confident that we've made A Year with **Yours** 2012 our best yet. So, a heartfelt thanks to all who contributed, including those whose letters we didn't have room to publish.

Happy reading – and all the best for 2012

Sharon Reid
Deputy and Specials Editor, **Yours** Magazine

Sunday **1** *New Year's Day*	**Thursday** **12**
Monday **2** *Bank Holiday*	**Friday** **13**
Tuesday **3**	**Saturday** **14**
Wednesday **4**	**Sunday** **15**
Thursday **5**	**Monday** **16**
Friday **6** *Epiphany*	**Tuesday** **17**
Saturday **7**	**Wednesday** **18**
Sunday **8**	**Thursday** **19**
Monday **9**	**Friday** **20**
Tuesday **10**	**Saturday** **21**
Wednesday **11**	**Sunday** **22**

Monday **23** *Chinese New Year (Year of the Dragon)*	**Saturday** **28**
Tuesday **24**	**Sunday** **29**
Wednesday **25** *Burns' Night*	**Monday** **30**
Thursday **26**	**Tuesday** **31**
Friday **27** *Holocaust Memorial Day*	

PIC: ISTOCKPHOTO

Poem of the month

Ah! Those winter nights

Cosy big fires heating the house,
Cat sleeping soundly, no thought of a mouse.
Mug of hot chocolate, scrumptiously creamy;
Feet in old slippers (not very seemly).
Hailstones beat loudly against window panes;
Footsteps rush homewards along muddy lanes.

How relaxing it is to be snugly inside,
Away from the coldness of winter outside.
The logs on the fire spit out red sparks
All over the rug, making little black marks.
The radio plays music (Puccini – so good!)
Wouldn't want summer back even if I could.

There's something magical about winter nights;
The gleam from the brasses shines in the lights
Of scented red candles in saucers of green
As shadows dance sprightly around the scene.
Oh! This den of tranquillity, all cosy and warm;
The passing of winter I will surely mourn.

Helen S Hughes, Little Neston, Cheshire

My Teenage Years
Jive Talking

When I visit our local theatre, I close my eyes and remember it as it was when I was a teenager and it was still a dance hall. Every Saturday night you'd find me and my friend Mary there, dressed in shapeless shift dresses and three-inch heeled stiletto shoes. Our hair was backcombed and lacquered, our eyes rimmed with black eyeliner and our lipstick was almost white. ("What do you call that shade?" Mary's mother asked. "Mortuary?")

In those days it was all live music and we danced mainly to local bands although some well-known stars such as The Searchers and Gene Vincent played there. We loved jiving. Mary led while I did the twirly bits. Occasionally, a lad would dance with us both, one in each hand, with two girls twirling simultaneously. If you were asked to dance and the bloke was useless at jiving, you beat a hasty retreat to the Ladies in case he asked you again.

Lesley with her Granddad Bert in 1963

There was no bar, so if you wanted a drink, you had to get a pass and go across the road to the pub, but we never bothered. We were far more interested in the music and the lads! Crowds of lads used to stand, leaning against the arched doorway, surveying the girls. There was quite often a fight, mostly between boys but occasionally a couple of girls would take each other on. It was quite exciting, but disgraceful behaviour really – certainly not the sort of thing that well-brought-up girls like us would indulge in!

Lesley M Bennion, Stafford

Bird of the week

PIC: ISTOCK

Chaffinch

Found all over the UK, the Chaffinch is a farmland bird that's made itself at home in our gardens. They're so confident they will often come to your hand for food. The male is the most brightly coloured with his blue-grey head, chestnut brown cheeks and back, and pink breast. A male proclaiming his territory by singing loudly from a bush top is one of the first signs of spring and, in fact, in the 19th century Chaffinches were caught and caged to take part in singing contests.
From Bird Watching magazine (www.birdwatching.co.uk)

Bright ideas

Don't throw away spice containers when you've finished with them. They make great sprinklers to decorate cakes and biscuits because of the small holes in the lid. Fill clean, empty containers with icing sugar, cocoa powder or even cinnamon sugar to add a touch of class to your cakes.

I wish I'd said that

"I've had a perfectly wonderful evening. But this wasn't it."
Actor and comedian Groucho Marx, was on top form with this witty one liner.

Only in Britain

The Haxey Hood

Dating back to the 14th century when a Lady out riding lost her hood to a gust of wind. Farm workers scrabbled to retrieve it and she decreed the fun be re-enacted every year. Today, on Twelfth Night, a large rugby scrum (called the 'sway') pushes a leather tube (called the 'hood') to one of four pubs in the villages, where it remains until the following year's game.

Our Tune

You Are My Sunshine – Jimmie Davis

My Dad sang this when I was a child, and told me that I used to walk down the lane leading to our farm, swinging my teddy bear by the arm and singing 'You Are My Sunshine'. It always reminds me of my childhood and happy times we spent together.

Anita Smith, Bury

Photo I can't throw away

This is my daughter and I having a New Year's Day splodge in our wellies on Redcar beach in January 1983. I made both these coats and they lasted quite a number of years, until she grew out of hers and I got sick of mine! I wouldn't part with this photo because it shows how happy we were, even though it was taken at a time when money was tight.

Sheila Camp, Spennymoor, County Durham

Recipe of the week

Super Healthy Udon Noodles

Serves: 4
Preparation time: 5 minutes
Cooking time: 10 minutes

- ◆ 500g turkey breast, thinly sliced
- ◆ 4 tbsp soy sauce
- ◆ 4 tbsp sweet chilli sauce
- ◆ 800g fresh Udon noodles, or medium egg noodles
- ◆ 200g pack sprouting broccoli
- ◆ 2 red peppers, sliced
- ◆ 6 small shallots, sliced
- ◆ 1 tbsp groundnut oil
- ◆ 2 cloves garlic, crushed
- ◆ 1 tbsp fresh ginger, grated
- ◆ Sesame seeds, to serve

1. Preheat the grill to medium and drizzle half the soy sauce and half the sweet chilli sauce over the turkey breast slices. Then grill for 3–4 minutes each side until cooked.
2. Meanwhile, cook the noodles according to packet instructions and set aside to drain and cool.
3. Slice the broccoli into 4cm (1 1/2 inch) strips. Heat the oil in a wok and stir-fry the broccoli along with the red peppers and shallots until everything is just cooked and slightly browned.
4. Add the garlic, ginger and the remainder of the soy sauce and sweet chilli sauce and cook for one more minute. Add the noodles and toss to mix well.
5. Serve the noodles piled high with the turkey arranged on top. Finish with a sprinkle of sesame seeds and serve immediately.

© Tenderstem Broccoli, www.tenderstem.co.uk

My Teenage Years
A penpal romance

When I was a schoolgirl in the Thirties, the term teenager hadn't been invented. I attended an all-girls secondary school where we were actively encouraged to correspond with penfriends from abroad. I volunteered to write to four correspondents: Jessica, an American girl; Gerda in Germany; and two boys, Jaromir and Alex who lived in Czechoslovakia.

Before the outbreak of the Second World War, Gerda wrote to tell me not to contact her again as she had joined the Hitler Youth movement and regarded an English girl as her enemy. Then I heard from Jaromir that his friend Alex had been drowned in a boating accident. By this time, Jaromir and I

Jean, aged 16

were conducting a kind of romance by post. The photograph he sent me was of an astoundingly beautiful young man and we found we had many interests in common, although his privileged background was very different from mine.

After war broke out, Prague became a very distant place in every respect and my only remaining penfriend was Jessie.

A footnote to this story came one evening shortly after the war ended when there was a knock on my parents' door. An unfamiliar voice asked: "Does Jean still live here?" Jaromir and I spent the following day together. He had been involved in his country's resistance movement and his youthful beauty was no more; he bore a scarred face and burnt hands. We reminisced before acknowledging with poignant regret that our futures lay in different directions.

Jean L Sealey, Belper, Derbyshire

Bird of the week

PIC: ISTOCK

Tawny Owl

Not often seen, except as a large shape flapping across a dark country road, the Tawny has given us the owl noise we all know – twit twoo. Actually these notes are the sounds made by two owls, the female calling the first, shorter note and the male answering with a long hooo. Tawnys are about the size of a Wood Pigeon, but with bigger wings. Their seeming ability to turn their heads backwards is due to their long, flexible necks hidden under abundant feathers.
From Bird Watching magazine (www.birdwatching.co.uk)

Bright ideas

If drinking glasses become stuck together when stacked here's a clever tip to separate them without breaking. Place the bottom glass in hot water, and pour cold water in the top one. Then, after a minute, twist gently and the glasses should part with ease.

I wish I'd said that

"You're as much use as a chocolate teapot."
A simple, yet effective, classic.

Recipe of the week

Only in Britain

The Whittlesey Straw Bear Festival

They don't come much stranger than this – a tradition that dates back to the 1800s where a man dressed as a straw bear is paraded around the town stopping at pubs along the way! The procession includes Morris, clog and sword dancers as well as musicians and entertainers. **For more details visit www.strawbear.org.uk.**

Our Tune

In the Mood – The Joe Loss Orchestra

Joe Loss and 'In the Mood' will never be dead as long as I remember dancing the jitterbug on a Saturday night. It didn't matter that I had to be home by 10.30pm, or that nylons hadn't reached Tyneside. The war was over and my teenage years were in full flow.
Pat Berkshire, Newcastle-upon-Tyne

Photo I can't throw away

This photograph shows me at about 9 years old with my paternal grandmother, with whom I spent many happy holidays. She had just picked me up from our weekly bus ride to the local town of Newmarket. I remember the Panama hat and pink cloth coat. My grandmother raised at least nine children, was a wonderful cook and always had love, time and patience for me, so this picture is a favourite of mine.
Sylvia Archer, Tenbury Wells, Worcestershire

Yogurt with Roasted Oats and Fruit

Serves: 4
Preparation time: 10 minutes
Cooking time: 5 minutes

- ◆ 100g jumbo porridge oats
- ◆ 2 ripe English pears, cored and diced
- ◆ 2 English red apples, cored and diced
- ◆ 500g low-fat natural yogurt
- ◆ 2 tbsp clear honey

1. Preheat the oven to 200°C/400°F/Gas Mark 6. Place the oats on a baking tray and roast for 5 minutes, or until lightly browned. Set aside to cool completely.
2. Meanwhile, mix the remaining ingredients in a large bowl and leave to chill in the fridge.
3. Just before serving, stir in the oats and drizzle with the honey.

◆ **Top tip:** Try serving in tall sundae glasses for a special occasion or try using flavoured yogurt for a different flavour.
© Wholegrain Goodness, www.wholegraingoodness.com

My Teenage Years
Seaside adventure

Edna (above) and Christine (below)
on the beach in Southport

When I was 12, I made a lasting friendship with Christine who was in my class at secondary school. She was brilliant at sewing and I was hopeless so she helped me with the dress I was making.

After we left school at 15, Christine got a sewing job and I worked as a book-keeper and typist at the Co-op. To make extra money, I cleaned the boss's car for five shillings and another man in the office paid me two shillings and sixpence for polishing his scooter. At weekends, I worked at a petrol station until I had enough money to buy my own scooter.

When we were 18, Christine and I went on my scooter for a weekend in Southport. We stayed at the Claremont hotel and went dancing at the Floral Hall opposite. I was invited out to a steak supper by a fellow scooter enthusiast.

Arriving back at the hotel at 1am, I rung the bell and hammered on the door, but no one came. It started to thunder and I was scared to death. Eventually, a man answered the door. He thought I was kitchen staff and told me to use the back entrance. When I told him I was a guest, he looked suspicious but let me in. In our room, I found Christine watching the storm through the window, worried about where I was. We saw the funny side of it, but we never returned to that hotel – it was too posh for us.

Edna Lydiate, Leyland, Lancs

Bird of the week

PIC: ISTOCK

Dunnock

The fact that this little brown bird is often mistaken for a Sparrow is not surprising when you know its alternative name is Hedge Sparrow. Unlike House and Tree Sparrows, though, the Dunnock is a ground feeder and shuffles around bushes and under bird tables without the bouncy hops and skips of other sparrows. It is one of our most promiscuous birds, with threesomes regularly seen, as well as a lot of partner swapping, all designed to ensure the survival of the most chicks.
From Bird Watching magazine (www.birdwatching.co.uk)

Bright ideas

Using a microwave for cooking? To ensure even cooking arrange the thicker part of your food on the outside and the thinner part inside. Also reduce the amount of salt, herbs and spices by half as microwave cooking enhances the flavour. You can always add more, if necessary, at the end.

I wish I'd said that

"Age is an issue of mind over matter. If you don't mind, it doesn't matter." **Mark Twain**

Only in Britain

Wassailing orchards

This lovely custom usually takes place on Twelfth Night, where traditionally local communities would gather to bless their orchards with offerings of cider to encourage a fruitful season. Sadly, orchards are declining and this custom is not so common, but it does still take place in some areas.

Our Tune

Help Me Make It Through The Night – Kris Kristofferson

My husband died in 1979. Our family were grown up, so it was very lonely. Each night I lay listening to the radio, and this song was sung several times. To this day I request it given the chance and, after 33 years, I still remember those nights and tears.

Catherine Hensley, Reading

Photo I can't throw away

In 1912 our local library opened and my Granddad became the first librarian. In 1914 he was called up to fight in the First World War. He'd be amazed if he could see the changes to the library nowadays. I've been researching my ancestors on the computer with the help of a library volunteer, and next year hope to find where my much-loved Granddad went in his military years away.   **Delia Haywood, Wakefield**

Recipe of the week

Light Lamb Stew with Rhubarb

Serves: 6
Preparation time: 10-15 minutes
Cooking time: 1½ hours

- ◆ 450-675g lean lamb neck fillet, shoulder, or leg, cut into 2.5cm (1 inch) cubes
- ◆ 2 tsp ground coriander
- ◆ 1 tbsp oil
- ◆ 8 shallots, peeled and left whole (or one large onion)
- ◆ 600 ml (1 pint) good, hot lamb stock
- ◆ 2 tsp light brown sugar
- ◆ 2 rhubarb sticks, roughly chopped
- ◆ 100g spring greens or kale, roughly shredded
- ◆ 2 tbsp fresh flat-leaf parsley, roughly chopped
- ◆ 2 tbsp fresh mint, chopped

1 Preheat the oven to 170°/325°F/Gas Mark 3. In a large mixing bowl, season the lamb with salt, pepper and the coriander.
2 Heat the oil in a large non-stick frying pan on a moderate heat. Cook the lamb in batches for 3-4 minutes, or until brown and transfer to a large oven-proof and flame-proof casserole dish.
3 Cook the shallots/onion in the frying pan for 2-3 minutes before spooning into the casserole dish. Then add the stock and sugar.
4 Bring the casserole dish up to the boil, reduce the heat, cover and transfer to the oven for 1½ hours, stirring every half hour.
5 Ten minutes before the end of the cooking time add the rhubarb and green veg.
6 Garnish with the herbs and serve with seasonal vegetables and rice or mashed potatoes.

© Simply beef and lamb, www.simplybeefandlamb.co.uk

My Teenage Years
Youth club larks

It was lovely to grow up on the large Cuckoo Estate in West London in the Fifties. We had a very good youth club held in the old Victorian school (where Charlie Chaplin had been a pupil). There was a large hall for dancing, a long corridor for table tennis, and big rooms where we sat around the fire and chatted. Under the building were 'the dungeons' to explore, if we weren't caught.

The girls played netball and the boys had a football team that we supported even on cold, wet Saturday afternoons. We went on camping trips to Denham where we swam in the river. We travelled there on a flat-back lorry with all our equipment (there weren't so many cars around in those days).

On summer days we cycled to Runnymead or to Ruislip lido to swim. We danced on the grass to a wind-up gramophone that one of the boys strapped to his bike; someone else carried the heavy old 78rpm records. Sometimes we met in an American-style milk bar in Greenford where we made our

Maureen and friend Pauline get ready for a cycle ride

frothy coffees last as long as possible.

Jazz clubs were popular, as were the local dance halls, the Montague in Ealing or Hoovers at Perivale. Another favourite venue was the Hammersmith Palais where we danced to the big bands of Ted Heath and Lou Preager. Dickie Valentine made his debut there and singers like Lita Rosa and Dennis Lotus were regulars.

Maureen Tutton, Aylesbury, Bucks

Bird of the week

PIC: ISTOCK

Blackbird

There are six million pairs of Blackbirds in Britain and they are found everywhere, from seaside to hills, farmland and woodland to parks and gardens, filling our early mornings with song. The name comes from the adult males, as the young males and females are actually brown, the latter often having spots and streaks on their breasts. The males' beak colour is important – orange attracts the most aggression from other males, yellow less so.
From Bird Watching magazine (www.birdwatching.co.uk)

Bright ideas

When you're cleaning the house, do the dusting, scrubbing and changing of sheets etc first and leave the vacuuming till last. This will give the dust time to settle and will mean efficient cleaning (and hopefully reduce the amount of times you have to do it).

I wish I'd said that

"I'd love to kiss ya, but I just washed my hair."
Bette Davis' cutting comeback as Madge in the 1932 classic The Cabin in the Cotton.

Only in Britain

Bognor Birdman

Every year crowds flock to Bognor to see human powered flying machines of all sorts launching themselves off the pier. Past entries have included penguins, doughnuts, vampires and even a skateboarding cow! **It's a great day out, to find out about this year's event visit www.birdman.org.uk.**

Our Tune

Never Be Anyone Else But You – Ricky Nelson

It was love at first sight when I met Alan. I was only 15, but there has never been anyone else. We celebrated our Golden Wedding anniversary last year. This song still brings tears to my eyes. It means as much to me now as it did in the Fifties.

Sylvia Southall, Penkridge

Photo I can't throw away

Most saturdays Mum went out to jumble sales looking for bargains. One time Mum came home with a lovely yellow dress for me. As soon as Dad saw me in it he said, "A sunshine dress for a sunshine girl." Dad had always called me Sunshine from the day I was born. Mum said it was only to be worn on special occasions, which it was, so I cherish this photo of me wearing it.

Iris Simmons, Hoddeson, Hertfordshire

Recipe of the week

Bramley Apple and Yogurt Fool

Serves: 6-8
Preparation time: 10 minutes
Cooking time: 15 minutes (Plus 1-2 hours chilling)

◆ 2 Bramley apples, peeled, cored and chopped into 1cm (½ inch) pieces
◆ 4 tbsp soft brown sugar
◆ Finely grated zest and juice of 1 lemon
◆ 50g dark chocolate, finely grated
◆ 10 sponge fingers
◆ 570ml (1 pint) ready-made, low-fat custard, chilled
◆ 450g Greek yogurt

1 Place the apples, sugar, lemon juice and zest into a medium saucepan. Bring to the boil, stirring occasionally, then turn down the heat, and cook for about 15 minutes or until soft. Add a little water if the mixture gets too thick. You are after a thick sauce, not a chutney. Leave to cool before putting in the fridge for 1-2 hours.
2 Grate the chocolate using a cheese grater, then pop into the freezer to chill.
3 Spoon half of the apple mixture into a large dessert bowl or 6-8 individual pudding bowls. Break up the sponge fingers sprinkle over the apple. Then spoon over half the custard and half the yogurt. Repeat and finally sprinkle with the chocolate and serve immediately.

© Phil Vickery for The Bramley Apple Information Service, www.bramleyapples.co.uk

Bootiful baby bootees

Takes
1 hour
30 mins

◆ Use contrasting ribbons or buttons to brighten up your bootees.

These pretty baby bootees are the perfect gift for much-loved new arrivals

You will need:

1 x ball of Little Knitting Company's Extra Fine Merino Wool Tebe in a raspberry shade
Pair 3.25mm (US 3) needles
1m of narrow ribbon in shade of your choice

◆ Size 1: Newborn
◆ Size 2: 1-3 months

Abbreviations

Alt – alternative; foll – following; k – knit; k1 – pass slipped st over; skpo – slip 1 st; sts – stitches; tbl – through back of loop; tog – together; yf – yarn forward to make a st.

With 3.25mm (US 3) needles cast on 30(34) sts.
K1 row.
1st row k1, yf, k13(15), yf, k2, yf, k13(15), yf, k1.
2nd and 2 foll alt rows k to end, working k1 tbl into yf of previous row.
3rd row k2, yf, k14(16), yf, k2, yf, k14(16), yf, k2.
5th row k3, yf, 15(17), yf, k2, yf, k15(17), yf, k3. 42(46) sts.
6th row k to end, working k1 tbl into yf of previous row.

2nd size only
7th row k3, yf, 18, yf, k2, yf, k18, yf, k3. (50) sts.
8th row k to end, working k1 tbl into yf of previous row.

Both sizes
K10 rows.

Shape top
Next row k18(21), k2 tog, k2(4), skpo, k18(21). K1 row.
Next row k17(20), k2 tog, k2(4), skpo, k17(20). K1 row.

Next row k16(19), k2 tog, k2(4), skpo, k16(19). K1 row.
Next row k15(18), k2 tog, k2(4), skpo, k15(18). K1 row.

Size 1 only
Eyelet row (k2, k2 tog, yf) 4 times, k2, (yf, k2 tog, k2) 4 times.
K2 rows.
Cast off.

Size 2 only
Next row k(17), k2 tog, k4, skpo, k(17). K1 row.
Eyelet row (k2, k2 tog, yf, k3, k2 tog, yf) twice, k4, (yf, k2 tog, k3, yf, k2 tog, k2) twice.
K2 rows.
Cast off.

MAKE UP
Join seam. Cut ribbon in half, thread through eyelets to tie at centre front.

The Little Knitting Company stocks lots more gorgeous patterns and knitting materials, call 07980 439 587 or visit www.thelittleknittingcompany.co.uk.

Quiz of the month

Test your knowledge of classic TV comedy?
If you get stuck, the answers are below

1 Name the actor who played Private Frazer in Dad's Army?

2 What was the name of Barbara's two pigs in The Good Life?

3 What does M*A*S*H stand for?

4 What is the name of the pub in Only Fools and Horses?

5 What was the surname of the family in Till Death Do Us Part?

6 In Some Mothers Do 'Ave 'Em 1978 Christmas special, what type of lessons did Frank take?

7 What were the surnames of the two couples in The Good Life?

8 In Are You Being Served? what was Mr Rumbold's first name?

PIC: REXFEATURES

The cast of Fawlty Towers – but where was it set?

9 Which war was M*A*S*H set in?

10 Which town was the Fawlty Towers hotel located in?

11 In Only Fools and Horses, the Trotters live in a tower block named after which famous South African president?

12 What are the names of the main characters in One Foot in the Grave?

13 In M*A*S*H what is the name of Hawkeye's tent?

14 In Porridge, what was the length of Fletcher's prison sentence?

15 In Fawlty Towers, what is the name of the elderly guest who is hard of hearing?

16 What was the name of the bus company in On The Buses?

17 What was Captain Mainwaring's first name in Dad's Army?

18 In On the Buses, what was Stan Butler's catchphrase?

ANSWERS – 1) John Laurie 2) Pinky and Perky 3) Mobile Army Surgical Hospital 4) The Nag's Head 5) Garnett 6) Flying 7) Good and Leadbetter 8) Cuthbert 9) Korean 10) Torquay 11) Nelson Mandela 12) Victor and Margaret 13) The swamp 14) 5 years 15) Mrs Richards 16) Luxton and District Traction Company 17) George 18) "Cor Blimey!"

A Class Act

BY: BOB BROADFIELD

Variety is dying – and Vince and Harry are feeling the pinch

The assistant stage manager at the Empire Theatre raised his eyes to the ceiling in a 'here we go again' look as the double act of Harry and Vince came off and walked into the wings, almost knocking him over as they brushed past him and the scantily clad dancers who were waiting to go on.

Harry, the senior of the two, could be heard ranting and raving as they made their way down to the dressing rooms. Vince didn't say a word as, for the second time that day, he watched Harry open a bottle of whisky. Not bothering with the nicety of a glass, he proceeded to swig it straight from the bottle.

The two of them had been together for more than 20 years. Harry was well known in the profession for his heavy drinking, which was a constant source of worry to Vince. Recently, he had been hitting the bottle harder than ever because it was the Fifties and across the country the death knell was tolling for variety theatres. With the growth of television – since the Queen's Coronation almost every home had one – their demise was just a matter of time.

The first house on a Monday night was enough to make a saint turn to drink. "How can I get any response from an audience of 22 people? And 15 of those are complimentary tickets!" Harry complained bitterly, only too aware that like the rest of the cast they were on a percentage of the box office. "And that so-called blinking comedian didn't help by cutting his act short," he added.

Vince rasped back: "You can't blame him with an audience like that. The way we were going I thought we'd have to cut ours as well."

Harry glared at him. "Okay! Okay! I know what you're going to say next!"

'I know what you're going to say next!'

Vince continued accusingly: "You've been guzzling booze for the past 18 years, but the smell of whisky on your breath tonight was the worst I've ever known – you almost made ME forget my lines."

"Why don't you change the record?" asked Harry wearily.

"And don't make that old excuse about first-night jitters. It's about time you got over those by now," Vince responded.

"It's not the first-night jitters, it's the uncertainty of this business that's really getting to me. We can't go on much longer like this – but how else can we make a living? It's the only thing we know. And admit it, you'd be lost without me."

"Oh yes, I'd miss this eternal bickering, wouldn't I?" Vince responded sarcastically. "And, while we're on the subject, I didn't care for the way that girl dancer was eyeing you up and down – although why she should show an interest in a hopeless alcoholic like you, escapes me."

Harry mimicked him: "And I didn't like the way she eyed you up and down! Oh, dear. No need to panic, it's just a little harmless flirtation – there's no danger of her coming between us."

In spite of their continual arguing, the two performers cared for each other. An affection born out of the mixed fortunes that are inevitable in show business, and years of touring all over the country bound them together.

"There better not be," Vince replied from his usual seat in the corner of their dressing room. This was the only career that he'd ever known, the only world in which he felt at home. He liked to think that he and Harry played an important part in entertaining the great British public. Harry had come from a poor background and the drudgery of manual work had driven him to find a more exciting way of life. He had gone on the stage and, after many years of hard slog, had eventually hit on a variety act that got star billing.

'We should create a different image'

Looking across at the other half of his double act, Harry commented: "It's time you had a new coat. In fact, I think we should create a completely different image for ourselves."

Vince remained silent; he had heard all this before. Yes, he did need a new costume. The one he had was threadbare, but it would have to wait until better times came along. Since the bookings for their act had dropped off, they were just about able to make ends meet – although Harry always seemed to find enough money to purchase a bottle of whisky. Vince silently prayed that the second house would be better, and that Harry would be sober enough to go on and do his stuff.

An hour later, the bottle of whisky was almost empty. There was a knock at the door. The call boy chanted: "Overture and beginners, please, Overture and beginners, please."

Harry rushed over to the door. "What's the house like?" he asked, almost pleadingly.

"Looks good," replied the boy. "It's just beginning to fill up."

He was right. The excitement and general hubbub generated by the audience percolated backstage. Their mood of anticipation even permeated the dingy dressing room. Suddenly Harry's whole demeanour changed. He snapped out of his gloom and became bright and full of resolve.

Turning to Vince, he smacked his hands together and said: "Right, let's go out there and slay 'em." And with that he picked Vince up, sat him in the crook of his arm and carried him out of the dressing room.

Vince remained silent. After all, if you're a ventriloquist's dummy, you don't get much of a say in things.

Wednesday
1

Thursday
2

Friday
3

Saturday
4

Sunday
5

Monday
6

Tuesday
7

Wednesday
8

Thursday
9

Friday
10

Saturday
11

Sunday
12

Monday
13

Tuesday
14

Valentine's Day

Wednesday
15

Thursday
16

Friday
17

Saturday
18

Sunday
19

Monday
20

Tuesday
21

Shrove Tuesday (Pancake Day)

Wednesday
22

Ash Wednesday

Thursday	Monday
23	**27**
Friday	Tuesday
24	**28**
Saturday	Wednesday
25	**29**
Sunday	
26	

PIC: ISTOCKPHOTO

Poem of the month

Love me, love my zimmer

Please say you'll be mine,
My silver-haired Valentine.

You make my zimmer go zoom
When you enter the room,
My pacemaker race
When I gaze at your face.

My dentures do a skip
Each time that we kiss,
And my bones all ache
Crushed in your embrace.

Tell me, will this be the start
(Or maybe the finish?)
When I look up and say:
"No sex, please, we're British!"

**Mrs H C Smith,
Great Clacton, Essex**

My Teenage Years
Ankle socks to stockings

Here I am (at the back on the right) pictured with my friends, Elizabeth, Stephanie and Tricia. As teenagers in the Fifties we spent most of our time wearing school uniform. Even when we were 18, we still wore ankle socks because the alternative was a suspender belt and stockings – there were no such things as tights.

We did wear stockings when we went to dances or socials (which were usually run by the church youth club or the Boy Scouts) and we took great care to make sure the seams were straight. We got all dressed up in homemade dresses made from material bought at remnant shops, using a Simplicity pattern.

Teenage style in the Fifties was restricted to uniforms

We weren't allowed to wear make-up so we left home fresh-faced, then went into the cloakroom to apply bright red lipstick and either green eye-shadow (for brown eyes) or blue eye-shadow (for blue eyes). Finally, we splashed some perfume behind our ears and on our wrists – either Evening in Paris or Californian Poppy. After we'd done this, we thought we were the height of glamour and very grown up.

But at the end of the evening, it all had to be removed before we went home.

Barbara Cox, Hexham, Northumberland

Bird of the week

PIC: ISTOCK

Blue Tit

One of our favourite garden birds, Blue Tits are famously the birds that used to peck open the tops of milk bottles to get at the energy-giving layer of cream. Interestingly, although they can tolerate and benefit from cream, milk upsets their digestive systems. Nowadays, Blue Tits are not only most frequent visitors to feeders but also the birds most likely to occupy our nestboxes. They even use nestboxes in winter, when dozens of them will squeeze into one box to keep warm.
From Bird Watching magazine (www.birdwatching.co.uk)

Bright ideas

Fresh bread can be a real bother to slice, as the crust usually crumbles at the first sign of a bread knife. To solve this gently heat your knife by running it under hot water — dry thoroughly and you'll be slicing through bread with ease.

I wish I'd said that

"You're very smart. You must have brains you never used."
A smart comeback for sticky situations.

Only in Britain
Up Helly Aa

This traditional Viking fire festival takes place annually in Lerwick, in the Shetland Isles. A procession of thousands march through the town carrying lit torches before gathering for the burning of a Viking boat, which is sent to sea. It's such a big event that the following day is now a public holiday... to allow people to recover!

Our Tune
Wake Up Little Susie – The Everly Brothers

It was 1957 – Mum and Dad had gone to bed, so my boyfriend and I cuddled on the sofa listening to Radio Luxembourg. Fast forward a few hours. It was 2am and we were in trouble. He had to push his motorbike two streets away before kick-starting it into life!   **Fay Littlejohn, Exeter**

Photo I can't throw away

I have treasured this image of my daughter, Andrea, for more than 40 years, as it reminds me of the wonderful personality she had at such an early age.

She was always happy, cheeky and cheerful. For one so young she had many friends and enjoyed nothing better than a chat on the phone.

I didn't mind the inflated bills as it gave me so much pleasure seeing the effort she put into her facial expressions during the animated conversations with her pals.

Gloria Gormley, Preston

Recipe of the week

Cheesy Fish Pot Pies

Makes 4
Preparation time: 45 minutes
Cooking time: 30 minutes

For the pastry:
◆ 225g plain flour
◆ Pinch of salt
◆ 100g butter, chilled and cubed
◆ 125g mature Cheddar cheese, grated

For the filling:
◆ 450g cod or coley fillets, skinned and cubed
◆ 200g cooked tiger prawns
◆ 50g butter
◆ 50g plain flour
◆ 150ml dry white wine
◆ 425ml hot fish stock
◆ 2 tbsp double cream
◆ 1 tbsp fresh parsley and dill, chopped
◆ Milk, for glazing

1 Preheat the oven to 200°C/400°F/Gas Mark 7. Sieve flour and salt together into a large bowl. Add butter and rub lightly in until it resembles breadcrumbs. Stir in the cheese.
2 Make a well in the middle and add about 2 tablespoons of cold water. Stir using a knife, until a soft, not sticky, pastry is formed. Wrap in cling-film and chill for 15–30 minutes.
3 For the filling, heat butter in a saucepan. Gradually add flour stirring continuously. Add wine, stock, bay leaf and season well, stirring continuously until the sauce is smooth and silky. Remove the bay leaf. Add the fish, prawns, cream and herbs and divide between four individual pie dishes.
4 Roll out the pastry to the thickness of a £1 coin. Cut 4 circles about 1.5cm (3/4 inch) wider than your dishes. Brush the dish rims with water and cover with pastry tops. Glaze with milk and bake on a baking tray for 30–35 minutes, or until golden brown. Serve with new potatoes and peas.
© Cathedral City, www.cathedralcity.co.uk

My Teenage Years
Footers and films

Having survived the London Blitz, I entered my teenage years. My friends and I enjoyed being able to play football and cricket on Hampstead Heath, which had previously been covered by army units, ack-ack guns and barrage balloons.

I'd passed the 11-plus and attended Christ's College Grammar School in Finchley. My parents were not well off and could not afford to spend clothing coupons on expensive school uniform. My brother and I did as many odd jobs (milk rounds, paper rounds, dog walking) as we could to help pay the rent.

Since the age of six, I had sung in the church choir. From this stemmed my first love of music, hymns and operatic arias. In my teens, I loved Mario Lanza and went to see him in The Great Caruso nine times.

Gordon enjoyed the escapism offered by Hollywood films

It was lovely going to the cinema and seeing all the wonderful movies from Hollywood; it took us away from the bombed city streets to a different world.

I wrote to all the famous film stars, asking for a signed photo. I also wrote to the USA asking for a penpal and received more than 200 replies! My mother and father were quite overwhelmed by the postman knocking on the door with sacks of letters.

All this came to an abrupt end when, aged 17, I was called up to fight in the war in Korea. At the age of 18, I was made a sergeant and spent the rest of my teenage years in the army.

Gordon Carter, Easingwold, N Yorks

Bird of the week

PIC: ISTOCK

Grey Heron

Poised at the side of rivers, estuaries, lakes, and even garden ponds, the Grey Heron is the most widespread predatory bird in Britain and Ireland, with more than 6,000 nests every year in England alone. A highly skilled hunter that enjoys fish, frogs and rats, it is equally happy in fresh and salt water. Somewhat unexpectedly, perhaps, but rather like its cousin the Stork, it nests in a collection of thick twigs at the top of a tree.
From Bird Watching magazine (www.birdwatching.co.uk)

Bright ideas

If you have cumbersome thick cookbooks that refuse to stay open at the correct page, get a heavy, clear baking dish and place this flat across the pages you wish to use. As the dish is see-through you can still read the recipe easily through the vessel.

I wish I'd said that

"They say opposites attract. I hope you meet someone who's attractive, intelligent and cultured."

Only in Britain

Hurling the Silver Ball

This ancient game wakes up the sleepy Cornish village of St Columb Major twice a year. As part of the St Ives Feast Day, a silver ball is thrown into the crowd and two teams battle for possession. The ball has found its way into pubs and even private houses in the past!

Our Tune

Unforgettable – Nat King Cole

When my boyfriend used to cycle through our village to call for me, he would whistle this song. The neighbours all said, 'He's letting you know how he feels about you'. When we married, they came to church to hand us a horseshoe and say how they'd miss him whistling!

Jean Neal, Choppington, Northumberland

Photo I can't throw away

At the age of 81 I look back with many happy memories of our netball days. We played in our lunch hour. As you can see, most supporters were men! I also played in a Saturday team, and we had a hilarious time travelling all over the country. Once, the coach driver was pulled over for speeding and tried to pretend we were the All England Netball Team! This photo was taken and published in the local evening newspaper in the Fifties.

Joyce Mears, Clacton-on-Sea

Recipe of the week

Chocolate Mint Fondant Sundaes

Serves: 4
Preparation time: 15 minutes
(plus 30 minutes chilling time)

- ◆ 175g chocolate brownies or chocolate sponge cake
- ◆ 150g After Eight mints
- ◆ 100ml (4 fl oz) whipping cream
- ◆ 50g half-fat crème fraîche
To serve:
- ◆ 75g half-fat crème fraîche.
- ◆ 4 squares dark chocolate, grated

1 Crumble the brownies into medium chunks and divide between four serving glasses. Melt the mints for about 20 seconds on low, in a bowl in the microwave. Then add 1 tablespoon of boiling water and stir until smooth and thick.
2 Take a third of the melted chocolate and spoon over the brownies. Next, whip the cream until thickened, but not too stiff and then fold in the rest of the chocolate and the crème fraîche.
3 Divide this between the four sundaes so you get layers of rich cake, dark chocolate mint fondant, and a lighter chocolate cream. Finish with a dollop of thick crème fraîche and a sprinkling of grated chocolate.
4 Cover and chill for at least 30 minutes and serve the same day.

◆ **Top tip:** Choose good quality chocolate brownies or cake for this recipe.
© After Eight, www.aftereight.co.uk

My Teenage Years
Paw-paws and rickshaws

When I was 12, in 1947, my family moved from Wigan in Lancashire to Durban in South Africa. Everything was new and exciting: the sub-tropical climate, exotic flowers, vast white beaches and the Zulu rickshaw boys.

Our house had a corrugated-iron roof and a veranda round it. My brother and I went barefoot and picked mangos, paw-paws and bananas in our own garden. We watched in fascination as chameleons changed colour but ran away from horrible cockroaches. I still have the scar from a tarantula spider bite.

At school we were taught the Afrikaans language while, at home, we learned Zulu from the house servants. Due to family circumstances, I left school at 15 and worked in a number of stores before being accepted as an assistant in a dental practice.

A boyfriend who had a car was prized (preferably a large American model) as this meant drives along the coast to an oyster farm, a game reserve or one

Kathleen still has the scar from a tarantula spider bite

of the huge sugar plantations. We made most of our own clothes from cotton bought in the Indian market. Everyone dressed smartly to go to the bioscope cinema or to concerts in the city hall.

One day, when listening to an orchestra rehearsing for one of these concerts, I met a young fellow who was an officer on a freighter lying in the harbour. I learned there was a vacancy in the catering department onboard and seized the opportunity to work my way back to England.

Kathleen Atkinson, Ramsgate, Kent

Bird of the week

PIC: ISTOCK

Redpoll

There are three varieties of Redpoll but the one we're most likely to see swinging from the seedcases in a birch or alder tree is the Lesser Redpoll, instantly recognisable, if you're reasonably close, by the red spot on their foreheads. These birds are easier to see in winter when the leaves are off the trees because, although they chatter to one another when they're flying in a flock, they tend not to make much noise after they've landed and are feeding.
From Bird Watching magazine (www.birdwatching.co.uk)

Bright ideas

If you get annoyed with steamed-up bathroom mirrors after a shower or bath, simply use a clean cloth to rub a drop or two of shampoo onto your mirror before jumping in to get clean. There'll be clear mirrors when you get out ready and waiting for preening purposes!

I wish I'd said that

Nancy Astor to Winston Churchill: "If I were married to you, I'd put poison in your coffee."
Winston Churchill in reply: "If you were my wife, I'd drink it."

Only in Britain

Pucker up

Kissing Friday traditionally took place on the Friday after Ash Wednesday. In Leicestershire this cheeky festival was originally known as Nippy Hug Day. It allowed schoolboys to kiss girls without fear of being rejected and, in some parts, if a girl refused the boy would pinch their bum!

Our Tune

Wind Beneath My Wings – Bette Midler

Waiting for a knee replacement left me in a rather low state of mind, but my husband, Dennis, never gave up on me. After my operation, when a visiting hospital DJ asked what song I would like to hear played, it just had to be 'Wind Beneath My Wings' for Dennis.

Gloria Dyer, Benfleet, Essex

Photo I can't throw away

This photo was taken in 1956 when my team won our first ladies' darts match. I am in the middle of the back row. The lady holding the cup is Lily Marshall, the landlady who started the ladies darts league in 1955. I don't know where she is now but I would love to hear from her. I would never want to lose this photo.

Phyllis Greenhalgh, Manchester

Recipe of the week

Valentino Tomato Tarts

Makes 4
Preparation time: 10 minutes (plus 10 minutes cooling)
Cooking time: 25 minutes

For the sauce:
◆ 2 tbsp sunflower oil
◆ 1/2 onion, peeled and finely chopped
◆ 2 cloves garlic, peeled and crushed
◆ 400g can chopped tomatoes
◆ 2 tsp sugar

For the tart:
◆ 400g pack ready–rolled puff pastry
◆ 225g Mozzarella, sliced
◆ 4x slices salami
◆ 1 egg, beaten
◆ Large handful of fresh oregano, ripped into pieces

1 First, make the tomato sauce by heating the oil in a pan and frying the onion and garlic over a gentle heat until softened but not brown, about 5 minutes. Pour in the tomatoes and sugar and bring to a gentle simmer and leave until slightly reduced, for about 10 minutes. Season well and leave to cool slightly.

2 Meanwhile, preheat the oven to 200°C/400°F/ Gas Mark 6 and unroll the pastry onto a work surface. Cut out four heart shapes about 10cm (4 inch) across. Spread over the cooled tomato sauce, leaving a rim of 1cm (1/2 inch). Top with the mozzarella and finish with a slice of salami. Brush the egg wash over the exposed edge of the pastry.

3 Bake for around 10 minutes, or until pastry is crisp, airy and golden. Serve warm scattered with ripped oregano leaves and love will be in the air tonight!

© Cirio, www.cirio.co.uk

My Teenage Years
First Love, first kiss

I met my first boyfriend when I was 13. His name was Bob and I was madly in love with him. He was a choir boy in our local church; tall with dark hair and brown eyes. When we said goodbye, he would kiss me on the cheek then, after a while, on the lips. My legs used to go weak. We used to walk for miles with his arm around me – and that was all we did do. I was heartbroken when he went into the navy.

At 14 I left school and went out to work, first in a factory and then in a cinema. I was 15 when I met my future husband. We were married at 20. Unlike today, there was no sex before marriage – which, to my mind, spoils the honeymoon! We were both new to the facts of life and enjoyed finding things out for ourselves.

As a teenager, I loved to dress nicely and was lucky enough to have an aunt who was a court dressmaker. She made all my clothes and I used to buy the material from the market for sixpence or a shilling a yard. Sometimes my friend Gwennie and I went by bus to Oxford Street where I bought fabric from Selfridges' bargain basement.

When I was 14 I had my hair permed with curlers on wires that burned my head. Before that, my aunt used to put my hair in curlers made from strips of rags.

Vera Hilton, Weston-super-Mare

Vera in 1935... she always loved to dress in style

Bird of the week

PIC: ISTOCK

Kestrel

This is the classic bird we see working the scrubby grass at the side of a motorway. Its ancient country name is Windhover, easily explained by its unique style of hunting. It is the only one of our birds of prey to hold itself in one place for any length of time, watching with extremely keen eyes for the movements of shrews and voles below. Small mammals are not its only food, however, as it also enjoys beetles and even earthworms.

From Bird Watching magazine (www.birdwatching.co.uk)

Bright ideas

If you find yourself the victim of someone who has left their chewing gum on a bench or a bus seat and find some stuck to your clothes, simply brush the offending gum with egg white when you get home. Leave for 15 minutes before washing the item as normal.

I wish I'd said that

"All that you are you owe to your parents – why don't you send them a penny and square the account?"

Only in Britain

Blooming bonkers

Years ago us English folk were a tad superstitious and actually believed that if you cut both ends off a loaf of bread the devil would fly over the house. They also believed that finishing off a loaf at the table would ensure the following day's weather was fair.

Our Tune

We'll Gather Lilacs – Ivor Novello

This tune always brings a lump to my throat. My Grandmother used to sing it beautifully while she played the piano. On her birthday a couple of years ago I switched on the radio, and it was playing this, her tune. I had a good cry then for my lovely Nan.

Lynn Turner, Eastleigh, Hampshire

Photo I can't throw away

This photo is of my friend Rita and me – I'm the one with the short skirt on! We met as young married women in 1960 living in the same rented house in the East End of London. We are still friends after more than 50 years and still live close to each other. This photo reminds me how happy and full of hope we were, having both just married. Sadly, we are both widows now, but have children and grandchildren to enjoy.

Jean Smith, Hornchurch, Essex

Recipe of the week

Good-for-you Breakfast Pancakes

Makes 8
Preparation time: 5 minutes
Cooking time: 6 minutes

- 150g self-raising flour
- 1 egg
- 2 tbsp clear honey
- 150ml semi-skimmed milk
- 25g sultanas
- 50g bran flakes
- 2 tsp vegetable oil

To serve:
- 4 handfuls of mixed fresh berries
- Honey or maple syrup, to drizzle

1 Place the flour in a large bowl and whisk in the egg. Gradually add the honey and milk and whisk to form a batter. Stir in the sultanas and bran flakes.
2 Heat half the oil in a medium frying pan and spoon four tablespoons of the mixture into the pan, to form four pancakes. Cook gently for 1–2 minutes before flipping over to cook for one more minute, or until golden. Repeat to make four more pancakes. Serve immediately with the berries and a drizzle of honey or maple syrup.

◆ **Top tip:** Try replacing the sultanas with chopped dried apricots.
© Wholegrain Goodness, www.wholegraingoodness.com

Frame your love

Takes
1 hour plus
drying time

Craft your
loved one this
sentimental
heart frame this
Valentine's Day

You will need:

A box frame
A collection of photographs,
images and mementos or
keepsakes
Hi-tack glue
Sticky foam pads
Self-adhesive picture
framing tape

1 Start by removing the white
mount board from the
frame and assemble your
collection of mementos,
without gluing, until they
resemble a heart shape in
the centre of the board.

2 When you're pleased with
the layout, start to glue all
your bits and pieces into
position. To give different
heights and really get
that 3D effect, use a
combination of glue for
some pictures and the
sticky foam pads for others.

3 Lastly, add any 3D items
such as seashells and
buttons over the top of your
images – don't use too many
though, so you can still see
the photos and mementos
underneath.

4 Leave the picture flat to dry
overnight. Then assemble
the frame and tape the
backboard in place.

For more great craft projects and
all your crafting supplies call 01202
596100 or visit www.hobbycraft.co.uk.

◆ Resize images
using a computer for
a small collage like this
one, or, for a dramatic
effect, use full-size
photographs and a
large box frame.

Quiz of the month

Soap operas have been broadcasting for more than 50 years, but how well do you really know them? If you get stuck, the answers are below

1 Who played the murderous Richard Hillman in Coronation Street?

2 Which soap opera is set in the fictional county of Borsetshire?

3 Which year did Crossroads come to an end?

4 What was the name of the first soap opera broadcast on British television in the 1950s?

5 In which fictional Australian suburb is Neighbours set?

6 What is the surgery called in the soap Doctors?

7 In Eastenders, how many children does Peggy Mitchell have?

8 What are the names of Kevin and Sally Webster's two daughters in Coronation Street?

9 What caused huge devastation to Emmerdale in 1993?

10 Which soap opera is set in Summer Bay?

11 First shown on the station's launch night, what was Channel 5's original soap opera called?

How many children did this famous landlady of the Queen Vic have?

12 In Coronation Street, what was the name of Jack and Vera Duckworth's son?

13 In The Archers, what is the name of the pub in Ambridge?

14 In which city was Brookside set?

15 What was Dot Cotton's first husband called?

16 What channel did Neighbours move too from BBC1?

17 In Brookside, what was Tim O'Leary's nickname?

18 In Coronation Street, how many times was Mike Baldwin married?

19 In Eastenders, how did Nick Cotton's son, Ashley, die?

ANSWERS – 1) Brian Capron 2) The Archers 3) 2003 4) The Grove Family 5) Erinsborough 6) Mill Health Centre 7) 3 – Grant, Phil and Sam 8) Rosie and Sophie 9) Plane crash 10) Home and Away 11) Family Affairs 12) Terry 13) The Bull 14) Liverpool 15) Charlie 16) Channel 5 17) Tinhead 18) Four 19) He crashed his motorbike into the launderette

PIC: REXFEATURES

March 2012

Thursday

1

St David's Day

Friday

2

Saturday

3

Sunday

4

Monday

5

Tuesday

6

Wednesday

7

Thursday

8

Friday

9

Saturday

10

Sunday

11

Monday

12

Tuesday

13

Wednesday

14

Thursday

15

Friday

16

Saturday

17

St Patrick's Day

Sunday

18

Mothering Sunday

Monday

19

Tuesday

20

Wednesday

21

Thursday

22

Friday **23**	**Wednesday** **28**
Saturday **24**	**Thursday** **29**
Sunday **25** *British Summer Time begins (clocks go forward)*	**Friday** **30**
Monday **26**	**Saturday** **31**
Tuesday **27**	

PIC: ISTOCK

Poem of the month
Springtime guests

A nesting box we hung on the wall,
Waiting for the birds to call.
A few fleeting visits were all we had;
Surely our box can't be all that bad?

Food and water are set close by
So fledglings wouldn't have far to fly.
A warm welcome awaits our guests
If they decide to build their nests.

Two Blue Tits came to our abode,
Near the hedge, away from the road,
Nine eggs were laid – we had a peek,
Watching their progress, week by week.

Sadly, only five of the chicks hatched out,
Keeping mum and dad busy flying about.
The day came for our babies to fly,
We didn't have time to say goodbye.

We hope our guests enjoyed their stay
And want to return another day.

Mrs Patricia Briggs,
Walsall, W Midlands

My Teenage Years
The icing on the cake

My first job was in a bakery. Aged 15, I left school on a Friday and started work on the Monday. I was one of three girls whose job it was to decorate the cakes. Our hours were from 8am until we finished, usually around 6pm. On Saturdays (which was supposed to be our half day) we also had to do the cleaning. This involved cleaning all the machinery and scrubbing the concrete floors which took ages so we often didn't get away before 3pm.

The pay was one pound, fifteen shillings and sixpence a week, out of which I used to give my mum a pound for my keep. I made a lot of my own clothes, mainly with full circle skirts, which I wore with cardigans that I knitted myself.

Whenever we went out, there was usually a crowd of both boys and girls. There were a number of military camps in the area where we went to dances. They sent transport to pick us girls up and take us back (unless, of course, we found an escort to take us home). There were also two cinemas near us. A seat in the back row cost two shillings (10p in today's money) and the

Mooneen (right) in her homemade skirt

programme changed three times a week. Or we could get together for a game of table tennis at a local youth club. If money was tight, we just went out for lots of long walks.

Mooneen Truckle, Salisbury, Wilts

Bird of the week

PIC: ISTOCK

Long-tailed Tit

If a small group of tiny birds swoop across your garden calling to each other in high-pitched tweets, chances are they are a family party of Long-tailed Tits. These pretty little birds build the most delicate and elaborate nests, that take more than three weeks to construct. They mix wool and moss and bind it together with spiders' webs, decorate it with lichen flakes to disguise it and line it with an average of 1500 feathers to make it warm and comfortable for the chicks.
From Bird Watching magazine (www.birdwatching.co.uk)

Bright ideas

Here are some simple hiccup cures from folklore. Place your finger firmly under your nose and press hard for 30 seconds. Or drink a glass of water from the other side of the glass, bending forward to do so. Finally, inhale enough pepper to sneeze, this usually cures the hiccups!

I wish I'd said that

"Careful now, don't let your brains go to your head!'

Only in Britain

Leap Year proposals

The notion of women asking men for their hand in marriage originates from Ireland, but supposedly it was Scotland that passed it as a law. A woman's marriage proposal was allowed on February 29 – the date which according to English law had no legal status. Men who declined were made to pay a fine.

Our Tune

Everlasting Love – The Love Affair

In 1967, my sister worked for the NAAFI and was marrying an airman. I was invited to a dance to meet their friends, and The Love Affair were playing. Six months later I married one of the airmen, and after 45 years this song, sung that night, is still our tune.

Susan Millership, Sleaford

Photo I can't throw away

This picture is of my sister, Sylvia, when she got married in 1950. I was the bridesmaid. She made her dress out of parachute material that was free at the time. She has lived in Canada for the past 55 years. When she emigrated my mum was devastated. Sylvia still works in a shop selling material – at 80 that's not bad going! She is an inspiration to us all. **Judy Lye, Bristol**

Recipe of the week

Aubergine and Tomato Lasagne

Serves: 6
Preparation time: 20 minutes
Cooking time: 50 minutes

◆ 2 tbsp olive oil
◆ 1 medium aubergine, finely chopped
◆ 1 onion, finely chopped
◆ 100g mushrooms, finely chopped
◆ 2 large tomatoes, finely chopped
◆ 500g jar tomato sauce for lasagne
◆ 6-8 dried lasagne sheets
◆ 500g jar white sauce for lasagne
◆ 100g Parmesan cheese, finely grated

To serve:
◆ Mixed leaf salad
◆ 1 ciabatta bread loaf

1 Pre-heat the oven to 180°C/350°F/Gas Mark 5. Heat the oil in a large frying pan and add the aubergine and onion, cooking over a medium heat until softened, about 5 minutes. Add the mushrooms and tomatoes and cook for a further 5 minutes. Tip in the tomato sauce, stir and bring to the boil. Then remove from the heat.
2 Tip half into a large 26 x 20cm (10 x 8 inch) rectangular baking dish. Arrange half the Lasagne sheets on top, then spread half the white sauce over them. Repeat the layers before sprinkling the cheese evenly over the surface.
3 Bake for 30-35 minutes, or until bubbling and golden brown on top. Allow to stand for a few minutes, then serve with the salad and slices of the bread.

◆ **Top tip:** Chop the vegetables quite finely – as if you were making a salsa.
© Dolmio Stir In Sauces, www.dolmio.co.uk

My Teenage Years
Dead fab boys

Scorching weather but Marion had to stay pool-side

A dip into my teenage diary reveals the usual saga of school (boring), boys (unattainable) and parents (didn't understand me). Apart from that, everything was 'dead fab'!

At the time I lived in Singapore and the swimming pool, visible in the photo, was the hub of our social life. This was where all the teenagers congregated every day after school. Sadly, for me, a serious ear infection meant I wasn't allowed to go in the water (I couldn't even swim) so instead of an 'itsy-bitsy teeny-weeny yellow polka-dot bikini', I wore a dress with at least four layers of nylon petticoats underneath. Fashionable, yes – but not ideal for temperatures soaring to a hundred degrees!

Every week, there was a 'teenage night' at the swimming club. We drank ice-cold Coke from curvy bottles and hoped not to be asked for a dance by the spotty boy in our class at school. While most of us gyrated innocently to the sound of Chubby Checker urging us to twist again like we did last summer, couples who were 'going steady' sneaked off to the nearby beach for a snogging session.

On another night of the week, the pool was turned into an open-air cinema with a screen rigged up on one side. We watched films made for American teenage audiences with stars like Tab Hunter, Tuesday Weld and Brenda Lee. Connie Francis singing the theme tune of Where the Boys Are still makes me nostalgic for those balmy evenings under a tropical sky.

Marion Clarke, King's Lynn

Bird of the week

PIC: ISTOCK

Magpie

Often much maligned, the Magpie is strikingly beautiful seen close up, when the black colouring on the wings reveals itself to be an iridescent purplish-blue and on the long, elegant tail as a deep green. A member of the Crow family, it is believed to be one of our most intelligent birds, with great ability for problem solving. Its bad reputation comes from the fact that it will raid small birds' nests for eggs and chicks, but this is really no worse than other large predatory birds.
From Bird Watching magazine (www.birdwatching.co.uk)

Bright ideas

These ironing tips will speed things up. Fold items with a pressed crease along the fold when drying to make it easier to iron. Cotton and linen fabrics are quicker to iron if slightly damp. Spray them with a little water if they have dried already.

I wish I'd said that

"Sometimes I wonder if men and women really suit each other. Perhaps they should live next door and just visit now and then."
Wise words from actress Katharine Hepburn.

Only in Britain

Beary odd

Oddly enough ancient British superstition tells that if a child rides on a bear's back he or she will be protected from whooping cough. Fortunately, for small children everywhere, bears are not so common in the English countryside these days!

Our Tune

The Loveliest Night of the Year – Mario Lanza

The weekend before we married in 1952, we went to the cinema to see a film in which Mario Lanza sang this. We enjoyed it so much that we decided to start our wedding dancing to it. Hopefully this month we can listen to it to celebrate our Diamond anniversary.

Lilian Irving, Wickford, Essex

Photo I can't throw away

In 1979 I dropped my daughter, Diane, off to catch the coach taking her dance team to compete in 'Come Dancing'. I was nearly driving away when Diane shrieked: "Mum! Can you backcomb? The hair stylist hasn't turned up." Of course, I leapt aboard the coach. Later, I sat awkwardly in my jeans among evening gowns and suits watching the performance. Diane, exhausted with excitement, rested her head on my shoulder after the team came off the dance floor. Magical.

Eunice Young, Stockport

Recipe of the week

Paprika and Parmesan Lamb

Serves: 4
Preparation time: 10-15 minutes
Cooking time: 15 minutes

◆ 4 boneless lamb leg steaks
◆ 2 tsp smoked paprika
◆ Salt and freshly ground pepper
◆ 50g (2 oz) butter
◆ 1 tbsp oil
◆ 50g fresh breadcrumbs
◆ 1 tsp dried chilli flakes
◆ 1 tbsp Parmesan or Pecorino cheese, grated
◆ 2 tsp Dijon mustard
To serve:
◆ Boiled new potatoes

1 Preheat the oven to 220°C/425°F/Gas Mark 7. On a large plate, mix the paprika, salt and pepper and dust the lamb on both sides with the seasoning mix.
2 Melt half the butter with the oil in a non-stick frying pan and sear the lamb for 2 minutes, turning halfway. Transfer to a plate and leave to cool slightly. Melt the remaining butter and set aside.
3 On a large plate mix together the breadcrumbs, chilli flakes and cheese. Brush the mustard over the top of each lamb portion, then sprinkle over the breadcrumb mixture, pressing down firmly. Brush the melted butter over the breadcrumbs.
4 Transfer these to a small roasting tray and roast for 5-10 minutes (for medium done) or until the breadcrumbs are crispy. Leave to rest for two minutes.
5 Serve with boiled new potatoes.
© Simply Beef and Lamb, www.simplybeefandlamb.co.uk

My Teenage Years
Leader of the pack

I used to be motorbike-mad – and mad about one young man on whose bike I rode pillion. When his attention strayed to another girl, I was determined to win him back. I decided the perfect opportunity would be the end-of-term school dance.

With great care, I bathed and dressed in a scoop-neck dress of white with blue flowers and a wide blue 'waspie' belt and layers of stiffened nylon underskirts. Gold stiletto heel shoes, deep blue eye-shadow, hair carefully groomed with golden glitter, and Devon Violet perfume. A friend lent me a gold and blue necklace. I was ready to knock him for six!

I spotted him as soon as I walked in to the school hall. Hardly daring to breathe, I waited for him to ask me to dance. I had many dance partners that night – but not the one I wanted. Disappointed, I went to the Ladies, then sat on a low brick wall, feeling sorry for myself. A voice said: "Do you mind if I sit with you?"

Not taking too much notice, I said: "No." Then an arm came across my shoulder – I turned, and there

Eve in 1961. Young love faded after she left school

he was! We spent the rest of the evening together. Like most young love, it died when we left school and moved on.

I recently met him again. Like me, he has aged. But unlike me, he doesn't remember every detail of the outfit I so carefully chose that night!

Eve Booker, Sutton-in-Ashfield, Notts

Bird of the week

PIC: ISTOCK

Wren

Not quite our smallest bird – that honour goes to the tiny Goldcrest – the Wren is, nonetheless, very charismatic as it flits around among our garden bushes trilling in its extremely loud voice. The male Wren builds a number of different nests for the female to choose from and he selects some very peculiar sites, especially those that have a strong smell like the lower branches of cabbage and broccoli plants, as well as places that involve fabric, like the old clothes on a scarecrow.
From Bird Watching magazine (www.birdwatching.co.uk)

Bright ideas

Crystallised ginger and other dried fruits can be a real pain to chop up as they tend to clump together and stick to the knife. Solve this problem by blotting a piece of kitchen towel with vegetable oil and rub over the knife blade before dicing as normal.

I wish I'd said that

"He has a face like a saint - A St Bernard."
Unknown author

Recipe of the week

Only in Britain

Pearly Kings and Queens

This heart-warming London tradition began in 1875 with a young orphan. Inspired by local street traders called costermongers, who wore decorative pearl buttons to attract customers, he created a pearly suit to draw attention to his charity efforts. These Pearly Kings and Queens still exist raising money for local charities.

Our Tune

Have I Told You Lately That I Love You? – Vera Lynn

My mum, aged 78, was dying of cancer. She wanted this played at her funeral. When Mum told Dad of her choice, he had tears in his eyes. Gently supporting her, the two of them danced slowly to the song as, with the greatest of efforts, Mum whispered the words.

Marilyn Walker, Hull

Photo I can't throw away

This is a photo of my grandparents. I never knew my Grandfather and my Grandmother. I remember only an old lady, although she was younger than I am now when she died. They were never well off, but this seems to be a posed studio photograph. I love her hat, which I expect would cost a lot today, and I envy her tiny waist. I think the photograph was taken to celebrate her 21st birthday – what a contrast to today's 21-year-olds!

Mrs M Wilkinson, Wigan

Clotted Cream and Lemon Cake

Serves: 8
Preparation time: 20 minutes
Cooking time: 25 minutes

- ◆ Butter, for greasing
- ◆ 225g butter, room temperature
- ◆ 225g caster sugar
- ◆ 225g self-raising flour (plus 1 tbsp)
- ◆ Zest of 1 unwaxed lemon
- ◆ 4 large eggs
- ◆ 4-6 tbsp lemon curd
- ◆ 150g clotted cream
- ◆ Icing sugar, for dusting

1 Pre-heat the oven to 170°C/325°F/Gas Mark 3. Grease and line two 18cm (7 inch) circular cake tins. Place the butter in a large mixing bowl and add the sugar. Beat until the mixture is very light and fluffy.

2 In a separate bowl, mix together the flour and lemon zest. Beat the eggs one at a time into the butter and sugar mixture, folding in a spoonful of the flour to prevent curdling. Then add the remaining flour to form a smooth cake batter.

3 Divide the mixture between the tins, and level. Bake for 25 minutes, or until the cakes spring back when pressed gently and are lightly golden. Leave to cool in the tins for about 10 minutes before removing and leaving to cool completely on a wire rack. When cool enough to handle slice each cake in half. Place one cake slice upside down on a cake stand. Spread with half the lemon curd, sandwich with another slice of cake and spread with all of the cream. Add the third layer of cake and repeat the lemon curd layer. Finally sandwich over the last cake half, sliced side down and dust the top with icing sugar.

© Rodda's Clotted Cream, www.roddas.co.uk

My Teenage Years
The Fifties were fun

As an era to grow up in, the Fifties take some beating. The country was still in jubilant mood following the Coronation and the futuristic Festival of Britain generated fun after the drabness of the war years. Our main source of entertainment was the radio and I looked forward to Norman and Henry Bones, The Boy Detectives, and Dick Barton, Special Agent. At work, we were allowed to listen to Workers' Playtime over the loudspeakers. Music was a top priority; we would rush to the record shop to buy the latest releases, then home to play them endlessly on our Dansette players.

In our local coffee bar, we'd hand jive to records on the juke box. One day, someone pushed the button for a Johnny Mathis song and from the moment I heard his wonderful voice, I was hooked. I joined his fan club and went to many of his concerts. I was also lucky enough to see the great Buddy Holly when he toured the UK in 1958, the year before his tragic death. The compère at that concert was the then little-known Des O'Connor.

Sylvia, aged 15, was a very fashion-conscious teenager

I was also mad on fashion, including accessories like clip-on flower earrings, lace gloves and feather headbands. I once spent nearly a week's wages on shoes.

I began dating a local lad but I have to admit it wasn't the lad that was the big attraction – it was the Lambretta scooter he owned. When he and the Lambretta parted, so did we!

Sylvia Lee, London

Bird of the week

PIC: ISTOCK

Song Thrush
Empty shards of snail shell next to a large stone are the giveaway that there are Song Thrushes about, as the birds crack open the shells to get at a tasty meal. Song Thrush chicks often leave the nest before they can fly, but their attentive parents keep up with their voracious appetites and ensure their safety even on the ground. Nostalgic British emigrants in the mid 19th century took Song Thrushes with them to New Zealand where they are now one of the most common garden birds.
From Bird Watching magazine (www.birdwatching.co.uk)

Bright ideas

If you find difficulty getting ramekins out of a Bain Marie with tongs without them slipping and falling back in; wrap a rubber band around each end of the tong and the rubber will help to grip the ramekins and allow you to lift out the ramekins with ease.

I wish I'd said that

"God is supposed to have made man in his own image. It would be a great shock to Christians everywhere if God looked anything like you, Baldrick." **From Blackadder to Baldrick in the popular TV series.**

Only in Britain

White rabbits

An old English superstition, saying white rabbits on the first day of the month was supposed to bring luck. It was once thought that black rabbits hosted the souls of humans, and white rabbits were witches. Rabbits' feet used to be lucky charms, but luckily for bunnies everywhere this has gone out of fashion.

Our Tune

Silver Wings In The Moonlight – Anne Shelton

During the Second World War, I was engaged to the love of my life – an air gunner in the Lancaster bombers. Sometimes I would look up and see the Lancasters – moonlight shining on them. I always remember this tune when I remember my love, who was killed over Hamburg in 1942.

Dorree Spencer, Lancing, West Sussex

Photo I can't throw away

This is a photograph of my Mum and Dad, Hylda and Jim Earley, at their wedding on the first day of Spring (March 21, 1931) in Moseley, Birmingham. I believe the dress, made by my Mum, was a soft, ivory-coloured material, worn with a beautiful, long veil and a feathery bouquet of ferns and carnations. My Dad also looks very smart! A handsome couple.

Sonia Stacey, Stratford-upon-Avon

Recipe of the week

Roast Pork Belly with Cheddar Mash

Serves: 4
Preparation time: 10 minutes
Cooking time: 2 hours 15 minutes

◆ 1.5 kg pork belly, rind scored
For the mash:
◆ 6 large floury potatoes
◆ 50g butter
◆ 100ml (4 fl oz) hot milk
◆ 125g extra mature cheese, grated
To serve:
◆ Steamed spring greens
◆ Good gravy, home-made or bought

1 Preheat the oven to 220°C/425°F/Gas Mark 7. Sear the pork well before putting, skin side up, on a rack in a large roasting tray and baking for 30 minutes. Then reduce the oven to 170°C/325°F/ Gas Mark 3 cook for a further 1½ hours, or until the cooking juices run clear and the meat is cooked through. Cover with foil if it gets too brown.
2 Meanwhile, 15 minutes before the pork is ready, peel the potatoes, cut each one into about six and place in a large pan of boiling water. Cook until they are almost tender, about 12 minutes, drain and return to the pan.
3 Add the butter and milk and mash until smooth. Stir in the cheese and keep warm until ready to serve. Leave the pork to rest for 15 minutes before serving with a good dollop of cheesy mash and the spring greens and gravy.
© Cathedral City, www.cathedralcity.co.uk

Sue, aged 15, leading the Conga

My Teenage Years
Too young for love

For me, Thursday was the best night of the week as that was when Mum and I went Old Time dancing at the Co-op Assembly Rooms. It wasn't every teenager's idea of a great night out but, back in the Fifties, it was mine.

And that was where I first found romance!

Being tall, I looked much older than my 15 years so when an 'older' man (probably in his twenties!) asked me to dance, I was very flattered. He was a lovely gentleman, in the old-fashioned way, so my mum thoroughly approved when he invited me to the pictures one Saturday night.

As I went to the local grammar school and had to wear uniform through the week, I was really excited to dress up for my first date. I spent the entire afternoon getting ready for my big night. Newly painted nails, hair done up tightly in rollers – nothing was too much trouble. At last it was time for our meeting. He gave me such special treatment; took me to the most expensive balcony seats and bought me a 1lb box of Cadbury's Milk Tray chocolates. I felt very grown-up.

Then he told me his parents had invited me to tea on Easter Sunday. I panicked! I was far too young for Sunday tea with parents, and all that this implied. I thanked him for a lovely evening and said 'no'. The next Saturday night, I was so relieved to just go to the coffee bar in town.

Sue Payne, Garsington, Oxon

Bird of the week

PIC: ISTOCK

Swallow

The first sign that summer is on the way is the arrival of Swallows on our telegraph wires. Their true name is Barn Swallow, hinting at their favoured nesting spots in farm buildings – sites that are becoming increasingly difficult to access as we move towards man-made materials for construction and away from draughty wooden structures with lots of nooks and crannies. Stretches of fresh lakes at this time of year attract diving aerobatic teams of Swallows skimming the surface of the water.

From Bird Watching magazine (www.birdwatching.co.uk)

Bright ideas

Silicone cupcake cases make great freezer containers for leftover sauce, stock or pesto you want to save for future dishes. Pour the sauce into the moulds and freeze as normal; because of the flexibility of silicone you can pop out the frozen goods a lot easier than an ice-cube tray.

I wish I'd said that

"Let's play horse. I'll be the front end and you just be yourself." **Unknown author.**

Only in Britain
Pooh Sticks

Pooh and friends were onto a winner with their favourite game. The World Pooh Sticks Championships is large event that takes place annually at Days Lock, Little Wittenham in Abingdon. There's lots going on and the game itself takes place on two bridges over the River Thames.
For more information visit www.pooh-sticks.com.

Our Tune
The Sound of Music – Julie Andrews

My late husband and I saw this film when we were courting, and were smitten with it. From that time I wanted to visit Austria, and eventually we managed it for our Silver Wedding anniversary. I still get a magic feeling every time I hear the music associated with it.
Christine Parsons, Leigh, Lancashire

Photo I can't throw away

This photo of my cousin Albert and me transports me back to 1947. I was four years old and my cousin was six, and we had been fishing for tiddlers. There had been an argument about who would have the tin. Albert insisted he should have it as he was going to catch the most, so I was left with the jam jar. We both caught two tiddlers each, so there was no fish for tea that day!

Megan Carter, Hillingdon, Middx

Recipe of the week

Banana and Peanut Butter Muffins

Makes: 12
Preparation time: 10 minutes
Cooking time: 20 minutes

◆ 200g self-raising flour
◆ 25g oats
◆ 75g light brown muscovado sugar
◆ 3 medium, ripe bananas
◆ 100g crunchy peanut butter
◆ 2 medium eggs, lightly beaten
◆ 25g melted butter
◆ 125ml (5 fl oz) semi-skimmed milk

1 Preheat the oven to 200°C/400°F/Gas Mark 6 and line a 12-hole muffin tin with muffin cases or baking parchment.
2 Take a large mixing bowl and sift in the flour. Then mix in the oats and sugar. In a separate bowl mash the banana and mix in the peanut butter, eggs, butter and milk. Stir this into the flour mixture.
3 Divide the batter between the muffin cases and bake for 20 minutes, or until golden. Leave to cool on a wire rack

◆ **Top tip:** These are ideal for breakfast on-the-go. Simply prepare the unbaked muffin mix and freeze in batches to use when required.
© Wholegrain Goodness, www.wholegraingoodness.com

Springtime blooms

Brighten up your home with this beautiful display created using an array of spring blooms and an old-fashioned jelly mould

◆ **Keep costs low by choosing a smaller mould and less flowers or use cheaper blooms.**

Takes 30 minutes

You will need:

An oblong traditional jelly mould, pie dish or modern stainless steel mould (roughly 20cm/8inch in diameter)
Chicken wire
Florist scissors
5 pink hyacinths
30 bluebells
25 pink tulips
30 grape hyacinths

1 Arrange a piece of the chicken wire inside the mould – this will give your flower stems support and help them stay in shape. Don't scrunch the wire up too much or the hyacinth stems won't fit through the holes. Fill about two thirds of the mould with water.

2 Arrange the pink hyacinths first as they have the biggest blooms and will help provide support for the other flowers. Insert one or two through the centre of the chicken wire and place the rest around the outside edges of the bowl.

3 Bluebells, tulips and grape hyacinths look better if they're grouped in small bunches. Fill in the gaps in the chicken wire around the hyacinths from the centre outwards with a few stems of each flower so they're massed together as injections of colour. Trim stems down so the tallest are in the centre, with shorter stems towards the edges to create a dome effect.

4 Prolong the life of your display by keeping your arrangement out of direct sunlight and away from radiators. On hot days mist your flowers with a spray of water to revive them.

Flower Arranging (£20), by Mark Welford and Stephen Wicks, published by DK, available from all good bookshops and online at www.dk.com.

Quiz of the month

Match these characters to the right costume dramas (there are two for each show). The answers are at the bottom of the page if you get stuck.

Lady Marjorie appeared in a TV costume classic

A Major Smith Barton
B Bella Seaton
C Aunt Fenny
D Louisa Trotter
E Jack Ford
F Tilly Watkins
G Lady Marjorie
H Mrs Elsie Hughes
I Mrs Bridges
J Mr Darcy
K Mrs Patmore
L Captain Ronald Merrick
M Lady Catherine de Bourgh
N Walter Monkton
O Jack Maddox
P Stanley Baldwin

1 The Duchess of Duke Street
2 Upstairs, Downstairs
3 Pride and Prejudice
4 The Jewel in the Crown
5 Edward and Mrs Simpson
6 House of Elliot
7 Downton Abbey
8 When the Boat Comes In

ANSWERS – 1) A & D 2) G & I 3) J & M 4) C & L 5) N & P 6) F & O 7) K & H 8) E & B

On the same

BY: BARBARA DYNES

Sally worries that her dad's hobby is taking over his life

Staring down into the innards of an old radio, Dad muttered: "Sal, I'm fine." I glanced around his living room. Old newspapers and dirty mugs littered the surfaces, bits of wire and electric circuit boards all over the table. Was Dad really coping? Okay, a bit of untidiness did no harm, but what worried me was the way he'd changed since Mum died – losing interest in everything except the old junk he collected.

Mum would have hated to see him like this. He used to be so funny, with his dry humour and quirky jokes. I tidied up a little, then we had a cup of tea. I left him happily rummaging in dusty old boxes for retro spare parts. As I drove home I told myself not to worry. Dad was healthy and independent even if he didn't get out and about.

I asked my husband, Craig, if he had any ideas. "What about the U3A?" he suggested.

"I've mentioned that. No deal!"

"Pity he's not into football."

Craig was sports mad; he couldn't understand my father's obsession with what he called 'all that rusty stuff'.

A few days later, Craig came home beaming.

"Just called in on your dad," he said. "He agreed to try the Scrabble club at the Legion Hall on Thursday!"

I blinked in disbelief. "How did you manage that?"

"I just said you were worried about him not going out."

"But – Scrabble?" I repeated doubtfully.

"Darren at work suggested it. His mum goes. And so do Fred Houston and his wife. Your mum and dad were quite pally with them, remember? So he'll see some friendly faces."

On Thursday, I drove round to collect Dad, prepared for him to make some excuse. Amazingly, he came to the door with his jacket on.

"Promised Craig I'd try it," he said.

"Great!" I smiled. "Remember Fred and Maggie Houston? They're regulars."

"Hmmm," he grunted.

I dropped him off and went home. Dare I hope that Scrabble was the answer to Dad's isolation? When I went to pick him up, I had a funny feeling that the evening was about to go haywire. I was right! My car refused to start.

I sighed. I could ring Craig, but it seemed unfair to interrupt his evening. I glanced at my watch. If I legged it I might make it in time. As I breathlessly hurried up the steps of the Legion Hall, I heard loud voices. In the group of people around the door I recognised Fred Houston.

"Of course there's such a word as 'bonzer'!" he was yelling. "It just wasn't in that small dictionary! Tom always brings in the big one, but he didn't turn up tonight."

"Just because you wanted to use your Z!" a familiar voice shouted back.

My heart sank. Trust Dad!

"What does 'bonzer' mean, then, Fred?" he challenged. "Bet you don't know!"

"Never you mind!" Fred retorted.

At that moment, his wife Maggie joined him. She grinned at me, raising her eyebrows in mock despair. Dad grabbed me by the arm and rushed down the steps, muttering that no way would he be coming back. I got out my mobile.

"I'm afraid my car's packed up, Dad. I'll ring for a taxi,"

Maggie appeared at my elbow. "We'll give you a lift."

Ignoring Dad's glare, I thanked her and bundled him into the back seat.

"Bonzer, indeed!" Dad leaned forward to make sure Fred could hear him. "You heard of that word, Sal?"

"Er, no." I didn't really care whether 'bonzer' existed or not. All I knew was that Scrabble was not the answer for Dad. Maybe he'd try something else? I glanced out of the window at the local allotments. Gardening, perhaps?

"Does it really matter?" Maggie was saying. "It's only a game! Anyway, how are you, Sally? Haven't seen you in ages."

"Look, I'll prove it!" Dad interrupted. "I've got the Concise Oxford Dictionary. Come in with me now and you'll see there's no such word!"

'What about the U3A?'

wavelength

'That's a Roberts, isn't it?'

PIC: KATE DAVIES

"Dad!" I protested. I loved him to bits, but my patience was wearing thin.

"Good idea!" Fred ignored me. "We'll settle it once and for all."

Maggie and I exchanged glances. We all trooped in and Dad made a beeline for his bookcase. "Here it is!" he yelled triumphantly.

"Coffee?" I inquired brightly, going into the kitchen. Maggie followed me.

"Men!" she groaned.

When we returned with the coffee, there was an eerie silence. I put down the tray and looked at Dad. His expression was unusually sheepish. "There is such a word," he mumbled. "Australian slang, apparently."

"Dad, I hope you apologised?"

"He did!" Fred grinned. "Great game, Scrabble!"

"Great, my foot!" Dad declared. "It's not my cup of tea."

I despaired. What, in heaven's name, was his cup of tea?

"I say, Harry," Fred took in the clutter on the table. "That's a Roberts, isn't it?" He inspected the old pulled-apart radio.

Dad jumped up. "Yes, from the Sixties – I'm trying to get it to work. You into this old stuff?"

"Don't ask!" Maggie sighed.

"Our house is full of ancient tape recorders, radiograms – you name it!"

But the two men, bent over the radio, weren't listening. "Come up and see my collection," Dad enthused.

As they went upstairs, snatches of conversation drifted down: "…Auctions and car boot sales… you must come… a crowd of us get together most Saturdays…"

I could hardly believe my ears. "Maggie, this is wonderful!"

She grinned. "It's just junk to me! 'Retro' they call it. I suppose that's in the dictionary?"

"Don't even ask!" I smiled.

April 2012

Sunday
1
All Fools' Day & Palm Sunday

Monday
2

Tuesday
3

Wednesday
4

Thursday
5
Maundy Thursday

Friday
6
Good Friday

Saturday
7

Sunday
8
Easter Sunday

Monday
9
Easter Monday

Tuesday
10

Wednesday
11

Thursday
12

Friday
13

Saturday
14

Sunday
15

Monday
16

Tuesday
17

Wednesday
18

Thursday
19

Friday
20

Saturday
21

Sunday
22

Monday **23**	Friday **27**
St George's Day	
Tuesday **24**	Saturday **28**
Wednesday **25**	Sunday **29**
Thursday **26**	Monday **30**

PIC: ISTOCK

Poem of the month

An Ode to spring-cleaning

Now that spring is in the air,
And flowers start to bloom,
As the sun starts beaming in
We look around the room.
The walls are looking dingy,
The paintwork doesn't gleam,
The carpet and the curtains
No longer look too clean.
We can't see through the windows
At the sunlight straining through.
The ornaments are dusty,
So we know what we must do.

It's out with mop and bucket,
And lots of elbow grease.
Soon all the house is shining,
It is a sight to please.
Now the day is over,
We view a job well done,
Then enjoy a well-earned rest;
Spring-cleaning has been fun!
**Mrs M Oliver,
Salisbury, Wiltshire**

My Teenage Years
Just a 'Rag' doll

Sue in 1961, aged 18

When I was 16, I entered a beauty contest run by our local paper and was amazed to be chosen as one of the six finalists for the title of Miss Luton. The final judging was to take place at Woburn Abbey. With the support of my boss (I was an apprentice hairdresser), I had my hair and make-up done specially for the occasion. With a new dress and accessories, I felt really special.

On the day, we were met by the Duke and Duchess of Bedford who took us on a tour of their stately home. As I was the youngest contestant, I was thrilled to be given third place.

Two years later in 1961, I entered the contest again. This time I was sponsored by the Vauxhall Motors apprentices' association. Although I did not win, I think that the four finalists had as much fun as the winner. On the first day of the apprentices' Rag Week, we formed part of a procession through the town, headed by the brass band of the Royal Marines. We had a police escort as rival apprentices had threatened to kidnap us – all part of the fund-raising fun.

During that memorable week, I met the TV newsreaders, Kenneth Kendall and Michael Aspel who were playing in a charity cricket match. Michael Aspel was sporting a black eye after being hit by a ball but, despite being in pain, was very charming. I also met the band leader John Dankworth at a charity dance.

Sue Stevenson, Chard, Somerset

Bird of the week

PIC: ISTOCK

Moorhen

The Moorhen is distinguishable from that other familiar black water bird, the Coot, by the red flash on its forehead and its yellow bill. Coots, by contrast, are bigger and have white faces and beaks. You can see Moorhens almost anywhere in the country where there is a pool of water, except mountain areas. Even a small flooded ditch can be home to these birds with their outsize, ungainly green feet. They co-exist with people very well, often using discarded wastepaper and plastic as nesting material.
From Bird Watching magazine (www.birdwatching.co.uk)

Bright ideas

If you suffer from rough hands, avoid washing them in hot water as this only aggravates the condition. Luke warm water will do; followed by a blast of cold water to close the pores and prevent dirt getting in, leaving them cleaner for longer.

I wish I'd said that

"I'd insult you, but you're not bright enough to notice." **A clever-clogs quip that won't leave you red-faced.**

Only in Britain

Marble madness

Story has it that the game of marbles dates back to Queen Elizabeth's reign, when two men from opposing counties played for the hand of a maiden from Tinsley – the site of today's British and World Marble Championships. More than 100 competitors take part and anyone can compete – so get practising!

Our Tune

After All These Years – Foster and Allen

The words to this song are beautiful and, being romantic, my late husband and I adopted it as our song. We danced to it at our 50th anniversary party. I often play it now but always end up crying. I loved my husband so much and my memories are precious.

Mary Bennett, Poole

Photo I can't throw away

Here is a photograph of my Dad, Leslie, in the RAF. He was a leading aircraft man in Cyprus. Here he is in the Sixties with all his RAF friends. Dad is in the middle – he was always the leader. He told me he had the time of his life in Cyprus, and always had many wonderful, gripping, heart-wrenching and funny stories to share.

Stella Robinson, Eastbourne

Recipe of the week

Minted Roasted Potatoes with Lamb

Serves: 2
Preparation time: 5 minutes (plus 30 minutes marinating)
Cooking time: 20–25 minutes

- ◆ 1 clove garlic
- ◆ 1 tsp ground cumin
- ◆ 2cm (3/4 inch) piece fresh ginger, grated
- ◆ 5 cardamom pods, seeds removed and crushed (optional)
- ◆ 2 tbsp lemon juice
- ◆ 2 lamb steaks or chops
- ◆ 400g new or salad potatoes, halved
- ◆ 2 tbsp olive oil
- ◆ 1 tbsp fresh mint, chopped

1 Preheat the oven 200°C/400°F/Gas Mark 6. Crush the garlic clove and combine with the spices, lemon juice in a large bowl. Add the lamb and season well. Marinate for 30 minutes.
2 Place the potatoes in a roasting tin, toss in half the oil and mint and season well. Roast for 20–25 minutes, or until tender.
3 Meanwhile, fry the lamb steaks in the remaining oil for 8–10 minutes, or until cooked according to taste. Transfer to the roasting tin for the last few minutes of cooking and serve immediately.
© Potato Council, www.lovepotatoes.co.uk

My Teenage Years
Those highs and lows

Here are some of my most vivid memories – good and bad – of being a teenager in the Fifties. I was a pupil at Liverpool Girls' College and our poor teachers struggled to keep our attention with all that wonderful, new, young music coming out of the wireless (as we used to call the radio). I caused hoots of laughter because I got muddled up and called Lonnie Donegan, Donny Lonegan. In those days, being the butt of laughter was painful.

In domestic science lessons, we made our own yellow tunics for PE. I also remember hand sewing a dress with a boat collar. The material was white with blue stars and the teacher admired my tiny stitches. Once I scored the winning goal at netball and was triumphantly carried off the pitch on the shoulders of my team-mates.

My family was quite poor and I well remember walking home in the rain and snow in my battered old shoes after singing in the choir

Growing up in the Fifties was one of mixed emotions

at the Philharmonic Hall.

I also wince when I recall the embarrassment of my first periods. As my mum couldn't afford to buy sanitary pads from the chemist, she made linen pockets from old sheets and stuffed them with cotton wool. I hated doing gym on those days of the month but the gym mistress was totally unsympathetic to my plight and said it was about time my mother got proper pads for me.

Betty Norton, Bamber Bridge, Lancs

Bird of the week

PIC: ISTOCK

House Martin

By now, these small, torpedo-shaped birds should be swooping around our roofs after their long migratory flight from Africa. With their blue-black and white plumage they can sometimes be mistaken for their close relatives the Swallows, but they have shorter tails and fly higher and with stiffer, flicking wingbeats. Like Swallows and Swifts they feed on insects in the air, but they are unique in their crafting of cups of mud for nests hanging under our house eaves.
From Bird Watching magazine (www.birdwatching.co.uk)

Bright ideas

Milk and dark chocolate chips have considerably less cocoa solids than a bar of normal cooking chocolate. So if a recipe calls for dark or milk chocolate chips finely chop up the required amount of chocolate from a bar for a tastier and better textured outcome.

I wish I'd said that

"His mother should have thrown him out and kept the stork." **American actress Mae West – well known for her controversial quips.**

Only in Britain
Coal carrying

Coal carrying is linked to the Sixties, when a bar-room bet led to a coal carrying race from a local pub in Gawthorpe, West Yorkshire. Today, the World Coal Carrying Championships takes place every Easter Monday in Gawthorpe, with competitors carrying a sack of coal weighing up to 50 kilos.

Our Tune
April Love – Pat Boone

My husband was in the Royal Navy and we were pen-friends, finally meeting on April 12, 1951. Of course our special song is 'April Love'. Four weeks later he was sent to Korea. We courted by post, married in 1953, and are still very much in love after 59 years.

Theresa Symonds, Bognor Regis

Photo I can't throw away

This group of bright young ladies were part of the Operating Department typing pool of British Rail in Glasgow. In this photo, taken in April 1960, we were on the annual office outing in Arran. As we weren't paid a lot and mostly lived at home with our parents, we didn't socialise much as a group, so the outing was always something to look forward to. I worked for British Rail for 16 years, and have lots of memories.

Margaret Underhill, Belper

Recipe of the week

Double Chocolate Fudge Cake

Serves: 8 - Preparation time: 5 minutes
Cooking time: 20-25 minutes (plus 1 hour cooling time)
Ready in 50 minutes (plus cooling time)

For the cake:
- 150g unsalted butter, at room temperature
- 150g light muscovado sugar
- 50g cocoa, sifted
- 150g self-raising flour
- 1 tsp baking powder
- $\frac{1}{2}$ tsp bicarbonate of soda
- 2 eggs
- 1 tsp vanilla extract
- 142ml (6 fl oz) soured cream
- 2 tbsp golden syrup

For the butter-cream:
- 200g white chocolate, melted
- 275g unsalted butter
- 275g cing sugar
- 1 tsp vanilla extract

For the chocolate curls:
- 100g (4 oz) white chocolate, melted
- 100g (4 oz) dark chocolate, melted

1 Preheat the oven to 180°C/350°F/Gas Mark 4. Grease and line two 18cm (7 inch) sandwich tins. Cream the butter and sugar. Then mix the dry ingredients in a bowl and add to the butter. Whisk the eggs, vanilla extract, cream and syrup and fold into the butter.

3 Divide between the tins and bake for 20-25 minutes, until springy. Leave for a few minutes, then transfer to racks to cool completely.

4 Meanwhile, to make the butter-cream, beat the butter and sugar together until creamy. Add the other ingredients.

5 For the curls, pour the melted chocolates onto a plate and chill until firm, not solid. Using a peeler, run the blade over to form curls. Chill until ready to serve.

6 Just before serving, Put one cake on a serving plate and top with half of the icing. Top with the remaining cake, then ice the top and sides with the remaining butter-cream. Decorate with the curls and serve.

© Nielson-Massey Vanillas, www.nielsenmassey.com

My Teenage Years
Hideous hot pants

I came from a large, low-income family, so my mother used to get vouchers to buy my grammar school uniform. One term, she let me have the money (around £25 – a small fortune) and I spent it on a full-length purple velvet coat. It was totally unsuitable for the Welsh valleys but I loved it and wore it to death.

I also remember wearing the most hideous hot pants. They were black, purple and yellow. I used to have to borrow clingy knee-length black boots from a friend to wear with them. I thought I looked fab. I never thought I had the legs for mini skirts but I loved suede coats with a fur trim and platform shoes.

I was very shy in those days. When I was 15, I had a date with a boy named Colin (who I really liked) to go to the pictures. I was scared that he would not pay for me so I begged some money from my sister to be able to pay for myself. As the time drew near, I grew more and more anxious. When I saw him walking up the road with a crowd of friends, I

Sue, aged 17, training as an army military policewoman

panicked and ran out of the back door and hid until he had gone.

I have not seen him for over 30 years but I want to say sorry, Colin, not just for hiding, but for making you look silly in front of your friends…

Sue Steel, Turkey

Bird of the week

PIC: ISTOCK

Woodpigeon

The rise in the cultivation of Rape Seed is thought to have led to an increase in our Woodpigeon population, as these fields provide an abundant supply of discarded grain to feed them. Their cooing song is one of the typical sounds of a spring or summer woodland walk. Woodpigeons are heavy birds, slow to take flight, so their strategy for deterring predators is to wait until they are close and then explode upwards with much noisy flapping – a strategy that doesn't work so well with cars!
From Bird Watching magazine (www.birdwatching.co.uk)

Bright ideas

Surprisingly, you can freeze leftover delicate herbs such as basil, dill and chives to save money. Simply chop them up and place into ice–cube trays and top up with chicken or vegetable stock. Use in stir-fries, rice pilaffs and soups for a great flavour kick.

I wish I'd said that

"You obviously overestimated my interest."
A good one to get you out of tedious conversation.

Only in Britain

Touch wood

Britain's favourite superstition is saying touch wood or actually touching or knocking a wooden surface. This strange superstition occurs worldwide, but, the British version dates back as far as the 17th century, when in Latin it was absit omen, which roughly translated means may there be no evil omen.

Our Tune

Night and Day – Cole Porter

I have always loved songs by Cole Porter, but 'Night and Day' is my favourite. I think it says what love is all about. Luckily my husband loved it too and we would often sing it together. It has everything a love song should have – music, passion and great lyrics.

June Davies, Cardiff

Photo I can't throw away

This photo was taken in 1960. I joined Billy Smart's Circus in my teens as a dancer/aerialist with Digger Pugh Aerial Ballet. We had to learn to ride horses and elephants, and do many other things involved in the circus. I am still in contact with some of the girls in the photo, and would love to know what happened to the others – I wonder if anyone else can remember the good times and fun we had.

Carol Uting, Beckenham, Kent

Recipe of the week

Pancetta and Butterbean Broth

Serves: 4
Preparation time: 10 minutes
Cooking time: 20 minutes

- 1 tbsp olive oil
- 200g diced pancetta
- 2 cloves of garlic, peeled and crushed
- 2 leeks, sliced
- 2 x 400g tins of butterbeans, drained
- 1 bay leaf
- 650ml (26 fl oz) vegetable or chicken stock
- 200g sprouting broccoli, cut into 4cm (1½ inch) pieces
- 1 heaped tsp Dijon mustard

1 Heat the oil in a saucepan and gently fry the pancetta, until lightly golden. Add the garlic and leeks and fry for a further 5 minutes, or until the leeks are softened.
2 Stir in the butterbeans and bay leaf. Pour in the stock and bring to a simmer. Using a potato masher, roughly mash the butter beans, keeping some whole but creating a thicker broth consistency.
3 Add the broccoli and mustard, and cook for 5 minutes, until the broccoli is tender. Season well and serve.

◆ **Top tip:** This warming hearty broth will go down a treat on a chilly spring day served with warm granary bread.
© Jo Pratt for Tenderstem® Broccoli, www.tenderstem.co.uk

My Teenage Years
A glimpse of stocking

Teenagers of today are a totally different breed from those of the Fifties when I grew up. Until I was 16, my main interests were sport and technical subjects such as woodwork, metalwork and technical drawing. Then I began to take more interest in Girl Guides than being a Boy Scout…

I became an apprentice printer and, although the money was not very good, I could afford to take a girlfriend to the pictures (with stern instructions from my mother to be home at 10.30pm).

Teenagers in the Fifties had more restrictions than today

Bird of the week

Great Spotted Woodpecker   PIC: ISTOCK

This colourful woodland bird is easiest to locate in spring as it announces its territory with a loud drumming, created by both males and females striking a rotten branch repeatedly with their beaks. Woodpeckers have long, sticky tongues to probe for insects under bark, and they also forage for nuts and berries. Increasingly, though, they find garden feeders provide an easy meal. Their toes are specially arranged with two pointing forwards and two back to enable them to cling easily to tree trunks – and feeders.
From Bird Watching magazine (www.birdwatching.co.uk)

I couldn't afford to sit in the circle (2s 3d) but we had a chaste kiss and a cuddle in the 1s 9d seats. If the usherette thought anything naughty was going on, she put a stop to it by flashing her torch along the row.

At the local hop, soft drinks were available and the dancing was quite sedate – apart from the jive when the occasional sighting of a suspendered stocking top would make all the boys sit up and take notice. My young lady at the time was carefully inspected by her parents before she was allowed out. If she had too much make-up on, it had to be removed, any unsuitable clothing changed (bra straps were never to be seen in public).

Even in those days there were rumours of certain boys and girls who had 'done it'. For me and many other lads, this sounded very mysterious and exciting, although we were never quite sure exactly what it was they had done!

Brian Hooper, Hornchurch, Essex

Bright ideas

Never put eggs for scrambling in a cold pan. The egg will seep into any cracks in the pan base and literally cook in the pan. Instead, heat the pan to a moderate heat so the metal can contract and seal any minute cracks.

I wish I'd said that

"In politics, if you want anything said, ask a man, if you want anything done, ask a woman."
Margaret Thatcher

Only in Britain

Sweeps Festival, Rochester, Kent

If you stumble across Rochester on the May Day holiday, you'll be sure to come across all kind of festivities as the town celebrates the traditional sweep's holiday. Expect a mix of dancing, entertainment and, of course, a sweeps procession complete with costumes and an infectious atmosphere.

Our Tune

Too Young – Jimmy Young

We married when I was 20 and Richard 22. During our courtship this became our song, because all our family and friends said we were too young, and Richard's reply was always: "We'll show them." We danced to it on anniversaries and parties for 53 years until my beloved died.   **Mary Quincey, Lincoln**

Photo I can't throw away

This photo makes me a little sad as I don't have my wedding dress anymore. We married in 1965 and my dress cost £25, which was a fortune to me as I only earned around £3 a week training as a flower maker. We bought a small bungalow and struggled with the mortgage, so I started making small items to sell. My wedding dress was sacrificed to make Cinderella dolls. But we did keep afloat, so it was worth it.

Pat Wells, Malvern, Worcs

Recipe of the week

Apple Brown Betty

Serves: 4
Preparation time: 10 minutes
Cooking time: 10 minutes

◆ 800g Bramley apples, peeled, cored and diced into 1cm (½ inch) pieces
◆ 75g soft dark brown sugar
◆ ½ tsp ground cinnamon
◆ 6 tbsp water
◆ 150g fresh blackberries
◆ 50g butter
◆ 150g fresh wholemeal breadcrumbs
◆ 50g oats

1 Place the apples, two-thirds of the sugar, cinnamon and water in a saucepan. Cover and cook gently for 5 minutes. Add the blackberries, and cook for a further 3 minutes.
2 Meanwhile, melt the butter with the remaining sugar in a large frying pan and fry the breadcrumbs and oats for 3-4 minutes.
3 Spoon half the apple compote into four wine glasses or serving bowls. Then spoon over half the breadcrumb mix. Repeat the layers and serve immediately, or leave to cool completely.

◆ **Top Tip:** This tastes great served with a dollop of low-fat crème fraîche or good-quality vanilla ice cream on top.
© Wholegrain Goodness, www.wholegraingoodness.com

Easter greetings

Takes 30 minutes

This blossom tree Easter card looks as pretty as a picture and is so easy to make

You will need:

Square white card blank or plain white card
Pearl green card or similar complementary shade
Natural raffia
Tissue paper in pink and white
Self-adhesive foam in yellow and orange
1 x 4mm googly eye
Small letter stickers
Glue
Scissors

1 Start by folding your blank sheet in half (unless you're using a pre-folded blank card). Cut and stick a square of the pearl green card to the front middle of your card leaving a small border around the edge.

2 Arrange your raffia pieces into a tree shape to the left hand side of your green card. Once you're happy with the shape glue this in place. To create the blossom scrunch very small pieces of the white and pink tissue paper and glue to the branches.

3 Cut a chick shape out of the yellow foam and then cut a round circle to create a sun. You can also cut sun rays out of the yellow foam if you wish. Glue both to the card, placing the chick in the right-hand bottom corner and the sun in the top.

4 Cut out a small orange triangle for your chick's beak and attach. Add two little legs using raffia and finish by gluing on a googly eye.

5 Finish by sticking on a lovely spring greeting using the letter stickers and then leave it to dry thoroughly before sending.

For more great craft projects and all your crafting supplies call 01202 596100 or visit www.hobbycraft.co.uk.

◆ **Make sure you buy an envelope that's slightly bigger than your card to allow room for your raised blossom.**

Quiz of the month

Put your children's television knowledge to the test by answering these multiple-choice questions. If you get stuck, the answers are below.

PIC REXFEATURES

1 What did the opening titles of Camberwick Green say?

2 Which year did Basil Brush first broadcast on British television?

3 What were the first words Annette Mills sang in Muffin the Mule?

4 What sound was playing in the background of the opening titles of Hector's House?

5 In Pipkins, what kind of animal was Hartley?

6 Which TV artist did the plasticine character Morph appear alongside?

7 Who was the voice of Torchy the Battery Boy?

8 In the Clangers, who is head of the family?

9 Who is the narrator behind the television programmes Trumpton and Chigley?

10 Who created the Thunderbirds?

11 In the Magic Roundabout, who played the guitar?

12 Who were Andy Pandy's friends?

13 In The Magic Roundabout, who said "time for bed"?

14 What did the Clangers like to eat that was harvested from wells by a dragon?

15 The firemen in Trumpton were called Pugh, Pugh, Barney, McGrew, Cuthbert, Dibble and... who?

16 What was the name of the little girl who bought strange objects for Bagpuss and his friends to mend?

17 If Rag was a hedgehog, Tag was a mouse, what kind of animal was Bobtail?

18 Where did Mr Benn go each week to start his adventure?

ANSWERS – 1) "Here is a box, a musical box, wound up and ready to play", 2) 1969, 3) "We want Muffin, Muffin the Mule", 4) Birds singing, 5) A hare, 6) Tony Hart, 7) Olwyn Griffiths, 8) Major Clanger, 9) Brian Cant, 10) Gerry Anderson, 11) Dylan, 12) Teddy and Looby Loo, 13) Zebedee, 14) Green soup, 15) Grubb, 16) Emily, 17) Rabbit, 18) Fancy dress shop

Three's a Crowd

BY: BETH CUNNINGHAM

Life in a retirement home is more fun than Betty expected

Mrs Thompson, manager of the retirement home, smiled at Betty and handed her the key to the snug little flat overlooking the sweeping lawn. "Welcome to The Willows. I hope you'll be very happy here."

As she unpacked, Betty felt sure she had made the right move. The bungalow and garden had become too big for her to manage without her dear John. Now she would have a simpler existence; social gatherings in the communal lounge, strolling through the park to the library, her radio and embroidery to keep her occupied in the evenings. What Betty did not expect was romance – or excitement.

The first surprise was her quickly blossoming friendship with Jim, one of the few men at The Willows and much in demand with some of the pushier ladies. But he seemed to prefer Betty's company. He helped her with a tricky jigsaw puzzle and saved her a front-row seat at the afternoon talk. Soon they were having the occasional glass of sherry at Jim's flat ,which was as neat and cosy as her own. Few men measured up to her John for old-fashioned courtesy and steadfastness but Jim, with a humorous twinkle in his eye, was delightful company and the perfect gentleman.

The second surprise was Imelda, who arrived at The Willows a few weeks after Betty. "Darlings!" she cried, bursting into the lounge one rainy morning. "Let's put on our wellies and go splashing through the puddles in the park."

She'd been a leading light in amateur dramatics and still liked to make a grand entrance. The stuffier ladies looked askance at Imelda, who dyed her hair red and wore jangly jewellery. Now divorced, she had no intention of growing old gracefully…

Betty found Imelda great fun and Imelda sought her company. "I'm so insecure underneath," she

Betty found Imelda great fun

confided over afternoon tea. "Absolutely lost without a man telling me how gorgeous I am. I wish I could be serene like you, Betty."

Imelda had a way of turning every little trip into a big adventure. As a threesome, with Jim, they had fun outings. When they went for a pensioners' meal at a local pub, Imelda persuaded the landlord to set up a karaoke session and did a brilliant impression of Shirley Bassey. For the tea dance at the church hall, Imelda dolled herself up in a flame-coloured gown and was overwhelmed by offers from ardent, if elderly, admirers.

When she was away, visiting her family, Betty and Jim resumed their gentler activities. "She's certainly a live wire, our Imelda," Jim observed. Betty hoped he wasn't finding life too tame in her absence. If he was, he was too polite to say so.

It was April and Betty's birthday was approaching. She hoped her friends would join her for a treat at their favourite teashop. To her surprise, Jim's response was lukewarm. And Imelda announced she was going to be in London. "But we'll do something when I get back, darling," she promised.

Betty felt hurt – but worse was to come. The day before her birthday, she spotted them in the high street. Imelda's arm was tucked in Jim's and they were gazing in the jeweller's shop window.

Betty hurried to the library. A happy explanation would be that they were buying her a birthday present – but that was unlikely. Only the previous week, Betty had told Imelda how John hadn't been able to afford an engagement ring but she had been satisfied with her plain wedding band.

"Poor darling!" Imelda had exclaimed. "Diamonds were the best thing I got out of my marriage."

So there was an obvious reason for Imelda and Jim's visit to the jeweller's but they didn't want to spoil her birthday by making their announcement too soon. Betty felt lonely for the first time since she had moved to The Willows.

Her birthday dawned grey and dull but Betty made the effort to dress smartly in her grey trouser

PIC: KATE DAVIES

Jim's first sip of coffee caused a coughing fit

suit and lavender blouse. As she was about to leave her flat, there was a knock at the door. Jim stood in the corridor wearing a yellow cardigan Betty hadn't seen before – and an embarrassed expression,

"Happy birthday," he said, a little lamely. Betty covered her confusion by asking him in and putting the kettle on.

Jim's first sip of coffee caused a coughing fit. He sank to his knees in front of Betty, grasping her hand. She was reaching for the emergency cord when Jim croaked: "No need, Betty. I'm just nervous and something's gone down the wrong way."

He groped in his cardigan pocket and produced a little leather box. Inside was the sweetest and plainest of solitaire rings.

"It's only small," Jim apologised, " but Imelda, bless her, came along to advise me and she insisted you wouldn't like anything flashy."

Betty fought back tears. Later – when they were wondering if Mrs Thompson would give them one of the spacious couples' flats on the top floor – there was another knock.

"Darlings!" shrieked Imelda. "It's been hell lurking in my room, pretending to be in London. I couldn't bear it a moment longer. I've taken the liberty of booking lunch at Luigi's. My treat. But first we must have a celebration drink."

She brandished a bottle of pink Champagne. Betty and Jim smiled at each other. Three would always be a crowd with Imelda around. And what a happy crowd they were going to be…

Tuesday **1**	Saturday **12**
Wednesday **2**	Sunday **13**
Thursday **3**	Monday **14**
Friday **4**	Tuesday **15**
Saturday **5**	Wednesday **16**
Sunday **6**	Thursday **17**
Monday **7** *May Day (Bank Holiday)*	Friday **18**
Tuesday **8**	Saturday **19**
Wednesday **9**	Sunday **20**
Thursday **10**	Monday **21**
Friday **11**	Tuesday **22**

Wednesday **23**	Monday **28**
Thursday **24**	Tuesday **29**
Friday **25**	Wednesday **30**
Saturday **26**	Thursday **31**
Sunday **27** *Pentecost (Whit Sunday)*	

PIC: ISTOCK

Poem of the month
Our bluebell wood

We climbed the hill; it was such a thrill
On that sunny day in May.
"Come on, Pam," shouts my friend, Jan.
"Just one more stile and we'll rest a while
Before we do more – as we are sixty-four!"

"You will be so glad you came,
And you'll never be the same
After you've seen the carpet of blue
Stretching through the woodland view."

A beautiful sight and the beautiful scent
Of heavenly perfume wherever we went.
"Let's take some photos to remember this day,
Best friends in the bluebells on the first of May."

Mrs Pam Sennitt, Swadlincote, Derbyshire

My Teenage Years
White boots and mini skirts

The Sixties was a great decade to be young – and they were not all about drugs and free love as people seem to assume. We had fun, freedom, and money in our pockets as jobs were plentiful.

The fashions were also great. There was the mini-skirt (the shorter, the better, according to the boys) and shift dresses, some with a slit up the sides. We wore white boots with our mini-skirts, with white lacy tights or fishnets. Towards the end of the decade, trouser suits came in and I wore a light green one to go away on honeymoon.

Hairstyles ranged from backcombed beehives to a pageboy style. We used to stick our fringe and side curls down with Sellotape to keep them flat and wore rollers to bed at night – very uncomfortable! The boys had sideburns and combed their hair into floppy quiffs.

Top of the Pops was launched on TV on New

Jenny in 1967, aged 17... the year she met her husband

Year's Day 1964, with Jimmy Savile as the presenter. At the time, the Beatles were still top of the charts with I Want to Hold Your Hand. But the song that meant most to me was Sailor, sung by Petula Clark, because when I met my future husband he had already signed on the dotted line to join the Royal Navy. I was 17 and ten days after our first date he left to start his training at Torpoint in Devon. We married in 1969 when I was 19.

Jenny Broe, Weston-super-Mare

Bird of the week

PIC: ISTOCK

Swift

The Swift is the small all-black aerial acrobat that famously spends the vast majority of its life in the air. As youngsters, the birds can spend three years permanently aloft, eating and sleeping on the wing, until they're mature enough to breed. They are responsible for the loud screaming calls as we sit out on summer evenings but, although we associate them very much with this country, they actually only spend a quarter of their lives here, from May to August.
From Bird Watching magazine (www.birdwatching.co.uk)

Bright ideas

If you need sliced strawberries to top a dessert. An egg slicer – used in the same way as you would with boiled eggs – is a great tool for ensuring perfectly even slices of strawberry. This also speeds up the process so you can spend more time eating the finished product!

I wish I'd said that

"It's better to remain silent and be thought a fool, than to open your mouth and remove all doubt."

Only in Britain

Garland Day

Many of you will remember May Day celebrations when you were a child and the tradition of crowning a May Queen. The chosen girl would lead the parade of May Day celebrations wearing a white gown and seated on a flower-decked chair. In some parts May Day was known as Garland Day.

Our Tune

My Moonlight Madonna
– Paul Francis Webster

In 1940 my boyfriend took me to the Manchester Ritz Ballroom. It was a frosty night but brilliant moonlight. Walking home, he said: "Do you remember that tune they played for the last waltz?" He told me it was 'My Moonlight Madonna', and that is what I was to him.

Margaret Poulson, Swinton, Manchester

Photo I can't throw away

This is a professional photograph of me and my brother, Gordon, taken when I was about three and Gordon was five years old. I came across it a few years ago and thought it was quite cute – especially Gordon in his little sailor suit! We were always close as there weren't many children in the village our age, so we made our own entertainment. People always said we looked alike – I think it was the hair!

Adaline Christie-Johnston, East Fell, Shetland

Recipe of the week

Black Cherry and Kirsch Desserts

Serves: 8
Preparation time: 5 minutes
(plus 2 hours marinating time)
Cooking time: 10 minutes (plus 2 hours chilling time)

◆ 350g black cherries, stoned and chopped (fresh or canned)
◆ 4 tbsp kirsch liqueur
◆ 1 tsp almond essence
◆ 200g good-quality dark chocolate
◆ 175g creamed coconut, roughly chopped or grated
◆ 100g vegetarian margarine
◆ 200g vegetarian almond crunch biscuits
◆ 50g hazelnuts, roughly chopped

1 Lightly oil eight ramekin dishes with vegetable oil and line with baking parchment.
2 Place the cherries in a bowl and pour over the liqueur and almond essence. Leave to marinate for 2 hours.
3 Ten minutes before the marinating time is up, take a large saucepan and melt the chocolate, creamed coconut and margarine together over a gentle heat.
4 Roughly crumble the almond crunch biscuits and stir into the chocolate mixture with the hazelnuts. Add the marinated fruit and any remaining liquid.
5 Pour the mixture into the prepared ramekin dishes and lightly smooth the top. Cover and chill for 2 hours.
6 Turn out the desserts and serve on individual plates with a drizzle of cherry sauce or a dollop of good-quality vanilla ice cream.

◆ **Top tip:** If you don't want to make this vegetarian use the same quantities of butter and normal almond biscuits.
© The Vegetarian Society, www.vegsoc.org

My Teenage Years
My first crush

I learned shorthand, typing and book-keeping at Dickenson's Commercial College in Preston. My grades were good and when I was 15 I started work as a typist in an insurance company. By the time I was 18 I was a private secretary.

My first crush was on my friend's brother. I longed for him to ask me out. When he did, I was delighted – but he didn't turn up. His excuse was that he lost his nerve!

Through helping to run a youth club, in 1963 I was chosen to represent Preston at a youth convention in London. We received an invitation to Lambeth Palace and I was one of the lucky ones who shook hands with the Archbishop of Canterbury. Unfortunately, when we went to Westminster Abbey for a service, I fainted and had to be taken out. We also went for a row on the Serpentine and to a show called The Bedsit, starring Spike Milligan. The end to our lovely weekend was a

Carole's first foreign trip was to sunny Italy

visit to Coventry Cathedral on the way home.

When I was 18 I went on my first foreign holiday with a cousin and two friends. We booked an Arrowsmith tour to Italy, flying from Manchester to Ostend and then by coach across Belgium, Germany, Switzerland and Luxembourg. It took 36 hours to get to our hotel but we had a lovely 12 days that included trips to Monte Carlo and Monaco. The whole holiday cost £34, all inclusive!

Carole Neville, Axminster, Devon

Bird of the week

Linnet

PIC: ISTOCK

A favourite caged bird in Victorian times because of its melodic song, the Linnet can now be mostly heard on scrubby waste-ground and commons where there are plenty of seedy plants and bushes. Sad to contemplate a single Linnet in a cage when you know that the birds are very sociable, preferring to travel in tightly bunched, lively flocks. Equally sadly, they are seen less often these days because a lot of their preferred habitat has disappeared under farmland, woodland and urban development.
From Bird Watching magazine (www.birdwatching.co.uk)

Bright ideas

Odd socks getting the better of you? Before popping a pair into the washing machine, fasten the toe ends with a safety pin. This way they will still get a good wash and never lose each other again!

I wish I'd said that

"Keep talking – I always yawn when I'm interested."
The perfect one-liner to excuse yourself from tiresome moments.

Only in Britain

Cheese rolling

This cheese lovers delight takes places in the quaint village of Stilton, Cambridgeshire, every May Day Bank Holiday. As bonkers as it sounds, hundreds of villagers and visitors flock to watch teams roll large cheeses along the high street. Expect fancy dress, entertainment and lots of cheese!

Our Tune

Where Have All The Flowers Gone – The Kingston Trio

In the Sixties, our rendezvous places were cafés. Everyone would sit around, talk over a soft drink and play records on the jukebox. My boyfriend always played this song. I haven't heard the Kingston Trio for many years, but this always takes me back to my early courting days.   **Daphne Williams, Caernarfon**

Photo I can't throw away

I treasure this photo of a school fancy dress competition in 1937 for the King's coronation. My Mother made my patriotic costume. I was dressed up in it when Dad came home from work and asked what my younger brother, Peter, was going as. Mum hadn't thought, so Dad sorted it, quickly getting a boxer's outfit together. I won first prize and Peter got second. A few years later our world fell apart when Father died and we were evacuated to South Wales.

Beryl Strawbridge, Caernarfon

Recipe of the week

Use–those–leftovers Turkey Casserole

Serves 2-3
Preparation time: 10 minutes
Cooking time: 1 hour

- 500g cooked turkey breast, diced
- 2 tbsp oil
- 1 onion, chopped
- 100g carrots, thickly chopped
- 100g celery, thickly chopped
- 600ml (1 pint) hot chicken stock
- 200g potatoes, peeled and cubed
- 200g frozen mixed vegetables
- 1 tsp cornflour
- 1-2 tsp gravy browning
- Warm crusty granary rolls, for serving

1 Preheat the oven to 200°C/400°F/Gas Mark 6. In a large saucepan, fry the onion, carrots and celery for 10 minutes, or until softened.
2 Add the chicken stock and season to taste. Place in an ovenproof and flameproof dish and add the cubed potatoes. Cover and cook in oven for about 30 minutes, or until the potatoes are cooked through.
3 Carefully remove the dish from the oven and add the cooked turkey and frozen vegetables. Return to the oven for a further 15 minutes.
4 Remove from the oven again and transfer to the stove on a low heat. Thicken the gravy with the cornflour and add the gravy browning. Serve immediately with the granary rolls.

© Change your meat not your menu, Bernard Matthews farms, www.bernardmatthewsfarms.com

My Teenage Years
Mods and Rockers

When I was 17 I was a Mod. I longed to look like Twiggy with cropped hair, lots of eye make-up and false eyelashes. My whole week was spent waiting for the weekend when I would meet my friends at the local club, The Black Cat in Woolwich, then catch a train into London. There were so many clubs in London at that time. We danced until the early hours to Ska or Bluebeat at The Scene at Ham Yard or The Flamingo in Wardour Street. (Georgie Fame and the Blue Flames were regulars at The Flamingo.)

Saturday nights were party nights and I can still remember the thrill of riding pillion on a Vespa scooter with about 20 mirrors attached to the front of it. A whole crowd of these scooters passing through the town drew lots of attention.

A club in St Mary's Kray used to open on Sunday afternoons. This was where we Mods met to

Ann with Jess, Terry and Pete

commiserate about having to go back to work on Monday. None of the clubs was licensed so the strongest drink we ever had was Coca-Cola.

Bank Holidays meant trips by train (or on the back of a Vespa, if we were lucky) to Brighton or Margate. My only worry during those days was that my older sister was a Rocker – and I didn't want any of my friends to see her on her boyfriend's motorbike!

Ann Rowe, London

Bird of the week

Whitethroat

PIC: ISTOCK

A summer visitor to railway embankments, hedgerows and thorny thickets, the Whitethroat sings all the time from perches as well as in flight. Walking along a country lane, you'll often find this small warbler bouncing ahead of you in short bursts of flight. Until the late Sixties it arrived in force, with numbers in summer comparable to the present population of Robins. However, it proved vulnerable to droughts in Africa in 1969 and 1984 meaning that today numbers are very much reduced.
From Bird Watching magazine (www.birdwatching.co.uk)

Bright ideas

Don't just resign onions to bulking up dinner dishes, they also prove useful for ridding you of rusty knives. Simply insert the rusty area into a large peeled onion for 5–10 minutes. Then move the blade in and out a couple of times and the rust will vanish when washed. Just remember not to eat the onion.

I wish I'd said that

"Frankly, my dear, I don't give a damn."
One of the most famous comebacks of all time – Clark Gable at his best in the 1939 film Gone with the Wind.

Only in Britain
Welly wanging

Where else in the world could hurling your Wellington boots count as a sport? Welly wanging, where you either throw or kick off your boot, is so popular that now official events take place across the country and championship events are organised all over the world.

Our Tune
Saw Her Standing There – The Beatles

I was just 17 when this Beatles record came out so, of course, I thought either John or Paul had seen me, with my bouffant hair, sooty-black eyes and Mary Quant dolly-rocker dress, and written it for me. After all, surely, 'The way I looked was way beyond compare'?

Sheila Pennell, Birmingham

Photo I can't throw away

This photo is of my older brother and I at Whitley Bay on holiday, when I was six and Ian was eight. I still remember how we enjoyed the pony cart ride, and I thought then how grown-up the lad in charge of the pony was. Sadly, Ian died aged 50. I am now in my early eighties, and this is one photo I can't throw away.

Mrs E McGookin, Alloa, Clackmannanshires

Recipe of the week

White Chocolate and Raspberry Blondies

Makes 10
Preparation time: 20 minutes
Cooking time: 30–35 minutes

- 150g white chocolate, chunked
- 100g butter, cubed
- 3 eggs
- 175g caster sugar
- 1 tsp vanilla essence
- 200g self-raising flour
- 1 tsp baking powder
- 175g raspberries
- 75g white chocolate, melted to decorate

1 Preheat the oven to 180°C/350°F/Gas Mark 4. Line a 18 x 28cm (7 x 11in) roasting tin with a large sheet of baking parchment.
2 In a small bowl, melt the chocolate and butter together.
3 In another bowl, use an electric whisk to blend the eggs, sugar and vanilla essence for about 5 minutes, or until it thickens and leaves a trail when the whisk is lifted.
4 Gently fold the chocolate–butter mix into the egg mix. Add the flour and baking powder. Pour the mixture into the lined tin and sprinkle with the raspberries.
5 Bake for 30–35 minutes, or until well risen and the top is crusty with the centre still a little soft. Once the tin has cooled, lift the parchment and blondies out and place on a chopping board. Drizzle with the reserved melted chocolate then leave to set. Cut into squares and peel off the paper to serve.

◆ **Top Tip:** Blondies and brownies taste better if slightly undercooked as the chocolate chunks will firm up slightly as it cools.
© Seasonal Berries, www.seasonalberries.co.uk

My Teenage Years
Skinny Lizzie

Being a teenager in the Sixties was very exciting but also very frustrating if you were living in a tiny village in rural West Wales. It all seemed to be happening in London and my friends and I wanted to be part of it!

We adored Top of the Pops and watched it religiously, trying to copy the dances we saw – like the Twist. I fell deeply in love with The Beatles, especially John Lennon, but my first great love was one of the boys in our gang, Brian. I followed him around like a lovesick puppy and dreamed of being kissed by him.

I was teased because I was so thin and nicknamed Twiggy. My girlfriends developed voluptuous busts while I stuffed cotton wool down my bra to make it look as though I had a bigger bosom. When the maxi and midi-length skirts came in, we all wore them and walked around thinking we looked great until our parents told us we looked like old ladies. The local lads wore flares or very

Elizabeth aged 14

narrow trousers; one lad had jeans so tight we wondered how he ever got into them.

When I was 15 there was worldwide excitement when Neil Armstrong became the first man to land on the moon. It was an amazing feat. After that, all the boys wanted to be astronauts. As far as I know, to this day none of them has ever made it!

Elizabeth Richards, Goodwick, Pembrokeshire

Bird of the week

PIC: ISTOCK

Barn Owl

Early evening over marsh land and grassy fields is the best time to see the ghostly pale Barn Owl patrolling in search of rodents. These birds are the size of a cat, but weigh less than 20 oz. They are found on every continent, apart from Antarctica, but there are fewer of them in Europe than there used to be. Their nesting sites have reduced drastically with the decline in old barns and wooden farm buildings and with the increased use of rodent poisons around human habitation.
From Bird Watching magazine (www.birdwatching.co.uk)

Bright ideas

Do you have leftover stale or soft crisps and biscuits? Simply place on a plate and microwave on full power for about 10 seconds. Leave to cool down completely before eating as normal. This only works once though so only microwave as many as you need at the time.

I wish I'd said that

"Some cause happiness wherever they go; others whenever they go." **Oscar Wilde – as sharp and witty as they come.**

Only in Britain

Woolsack racing

Compared to coal carrying, woolsack racing sounds a bit, well, woolly. But woolsacks weigh 60lb for men and 35lb for women and races are uphill! This unusual tradition began in the 17th century when local men attempted to impress local lasses with their woolsack carrying antics.

Our Tune

Walking Back To Happiness – Helen Shapiro

This song was in a pantomime I acted in, for which my husband was stage manager. Two of us girls had a bet as to which one of us could get him to take us out, and I won. We married in 1964 and are still together 48 years later.

Margaret Samuel, Bathgate, West Lothian

Photo I can't throw away

Family holidays on the Yorkshire coast were so enjoyable. Everything seemed calmer and happier in the Sixties. Walking on the promenade, we were told to dodge Mr Happy Snapper, the local photographer who seemed to appear from nowhere. Mum used to say, "That's another photo we'll have to buy!" But that's all we have to remember, so I'm glad Mum kept them in her little box of treasures.

Sylvia Foster, Bridlington

Recipe of the week

Brunch Omelette

Serves: 4
Preparation time: 5–6 minutes
Cooking time: 10 minutes

- 100g baby new potatoes, thickly sliced
- 1 tbsp butter
- 4 slices smoked back bacon or ham, chopped
- 200g mushrooms, sliced
- 4 medium eggs, beaten
- 3 tbsp semi-skimmed milk
- 1 tomato, thinly sliced
- Fresh green salad leaves, to serve

1 Preheat the grill to a medium heat. In a large saucepan of boiling water, add the potatoes for 5–6 minutes, or until tender, then drain.
2 Meanwhile, heat the butter in a small non-stick frying pan approximately 20cm (8 inch) in diameter and fry the bacon for 2 minutes. Then add the mushrooms and fry for 3 minutes. Stir in the warm potatoes.
3 Whisk the eggs and milk together, season well and pour into the frying pan. Cook on a low heat for 3–4 minutes loosening the edges with a spatula. Then place under a preheated grill for 2–3 minutes – adding the tomatoes for the last minute – until the top is golden and the omelette is cooked through. Leave to cool slightly before turning out of the pan.

◆ **Top tips:** Allow to chill before cutting into wedges for a great breakfast on-the-go. For a veggie option omit the bacon and sprinkle over 50g (2 oz) grated Cheddar cheese.
© Wholegrain Goodness, www.wholegraingoodness.com

My Teenage Years
Rock chick

My young life changed for ever the first time I heard Elvis Presley singing Heartbreak Hotel on Radio Luxembourg. I was transfixed – and after that I was really into the rock 'n' roll music scene that was sweeping the country. Among the stars that I saw at the Empire Theatre in Leeds were Cliff Richard, Gene Vincent and Eddie Cochran. They always put on a fabulous show. I also adored the late, great Sam Cooke. Even now when I hear him singing, the hairs stand up on the back of my neck.

Then along came the Beatles!

I first saw them at the Queen's Hall. My friend Kath (on the left in the photo) and I stood for more than two hours waiting for them to come on. It was standing-room only and the place was heaving, but we managed to push our way through to the front. It was all too much for Kath – the minute that they walked on to the stage – she passed out and fell on the floor.

I will never know how she didn't get trampled to

Jacqui (right) never heard a word the Beatles sang live

death. I helped her up and we had to push our way back through the crowd to reach the first aid stand. We missed the first half of the concert and stood at the back for the second half. The screaming was deafening and we couldn't hear a word they were singing but just to see Paul McCartney in the flesh was a dream come true for me.

Jacqui Harrison, Sheffield

Bird of the week

PIC: ISTOCK

Chiffchaff

These tiny birds, about the size of a Blue Tit, are among the first of our migratory birds to return in spring. Being browny-green and buff in colour, they are hard to distinguish from other small brown birds such as Willow Warblers. Their name reflects their song, which is a singsong ziff zaff ziff zaff alternating with the opposite zaff ziff every now and then. Chiffchaffs eat insects, which is bad news for aphids but good news for rose growers!

From Bird Watching magazine (www.birdwatching.co.uk)

Bright ideas

Befuddled by the world of wine? Generally, the rule is white meat, white wine, and red meat, red wine. However, rosé wine goes well with light-flavoured fish and white meat, along with rice dishes, cheese and bread. As it's slightly sweeter though, it doesn't complement spicy foods well.

I wish I'd said that

"If the saying, 'What you don't know can't hurt you' is true, you must be practically invulnerable."
Unknown author.

Only in Britain

Unlikely lucky charms

They were a superstitious bunch during the Elizabethan era. Some of the stranger ones included spitting into a fire, touching a man about to be executed or allowing a cow to breathe on you – all said to bring good luck!

Our Tune

Time After Time – Frank Sinatra

My husband and I married in 1947, and honeymooned in Torquay. We went to the local cinema to see 'It Happened in Brooklyn', in which Frank Sinatra sang 'Time After Time'. From that day it was our song, and whenever I hear it I still go weak at the knees.

Thora Baker, Melling, Merseyside

Photo I can't throw away

This is a photo of myself, in the dark skirt, and my old friend Freda, taken in the Fifties on the seafront in Sheerness, Isle of Sheppey. We used to go everywhere together, and are still best of friends. We both worked in the same grocery shop in the days when everything had to be weighed and bagged up, but we enjoyed it, talking to the customers as we worked. Those were very happy days.

Pat Smith, Weymouth

Recipe of the week

Pineapple Spice Scones

Makes 12 scones
Preparation time: 15 minutes
Cooking time: 12–15 minutes

- 350g plain flour (plus extra for kneading)
- 75g caster sugar (plus 1 tbsp extra)
- $2^1/_4$ tsp baking powder
- $^1/_2$ tsp baking soda
- 100g butter, softened
- 227g can pineapple chunks in juice
- 1 tsp vanilla extract
- Milk, for brushing
- 3 tbsp almonds, finely chopped
- $^1/_2$ tsp ground cinnamon

1 Preheat the oven to 200°C/400°F/Gas Mark 6 and grease a baking tray. Take a large mixing bowl and add the flour, sugar, baking powder, baking soda. Add a pinch of salt and rub in the butter until the mixture resembles coarse bread crumbs.

2 Make a well in the centre and add the pineapple chunks still in their juice and vanilla. Stir gently into the dry ingredients until they are just mixed.

3 On a lightly floured surface, knead the dough gently and pat into a 1 cm ($^1/_2$ inch) thickness. Cut out 12 scones with a floured 6cm ($2^1/_{2}$ inch) cutter.

4 Place on a greased baking sheet and brush the tops with a little milk. Combine the almonds, remaining tablespoon sugar and cinnamon. Sprinkle evenly over tops of scones and bake for 12 to 15 minutes, or until golden brown on top. Serve warm with a spoonful of clotted cream.

© Dole, www.dole.co.uk

Terrific tiger

Takes 30 minutes

This adorable tiger is just grrreat!

You will need:

35g orange sugarpaste
Small pieces of black, white and pink sugarpaste
Candy stick (from sweetshops nationwide)
Thin palette knife (available from sugarcraft and art shops)
Cocktail stick
Heart cutter, 2.5cm (1 inch)
Sharp pointed scissors

1 Divide the orange sugarpaste, taking about 20g for the body and form this into a long, pointed oval. Cut into both ends to form leg shapes. Mark the toes with a cocktail stick and push in the candy stick (broken in half) at the top of the front legs to support the head.

2 Divide the rest of the paste into two – a large pea size for the tail and what's left for the head. Roll the tail into a long sausage shape and make a ball shape for the head.

3 Make stripes from the remaining black sugarpaste by rolling very thin, pointed sausages 2cm (3/4inch) long. Stick them across the body, legs, tail and head (as shown). Attach the tail by squishing it onto the body.

4 To make the face, cut out a black heart with the heart cutter and flatten the edges slightly to widen it. Cut out a white heart of the same size and press on top of the black one, so the edge of the black still shows. Stick onto the head.

5 Attach two small white ovals for the cheeks, a small black triangle for the nose, and two tiny black eyes. Use a cocktail stick to mark whisker dimples on the cheeks. Stick the head on to the body, by spearing it onto your candy stick. For the ears, make two small balls of black and two smaller balls of white. Press the white gently onto the black.

6 Make two small sausages of white and flatten along the edges by pinching between your thumb and finger. Join the fat edge down the sides of the head and then make snips along the outer edges using the scissors to make them look fluffy.

7 Add back paws by rolling two small balls of pink sugarpaste and six smaller balls (three toes for each foot) flatten and stick in place.

◆ Use a small paintbrush and a little water to 'glue' items in place

Sugar Animals (£4.99) by Frances McNaughton and published by Search Press is part of the Twenty to Make easy craft series, call 01892 510850 or visit www.searchpress.com.

Can you match the characters to the science fiction programmes (there are two characters for each programme)? The answers are at the bottom of the page if you get stuck.

An enterprising poser for this particular captain...

A Craig Stirling
B Captain Troy Tempest
C Dr John Robinson
D Captain Kirk
E Dalek
F Lady Penelope
G Mr Spock
H Dr Anthony Newman
I The Major
J Captain Buck Rodgers
K Number Six
L Jeff Tracy
M Colonel Wilma Deering
N Dr Douglas Phillips
O Commander Sam Shore
P Sharron Macready
Q The Butler
R Major Don West

1 Dr Who
2 The Champions
3 The Prisoner
4 Thunderbirds
5 Stingray
6 Lost in Space
7 The Time Tunnel
8 Star Trek
9 Buck Rodgers

ANSWERS: 1) E & I 2) A & P 3) K & Q 4) F & L 5) B & O 6) C & R 7) H & N 8) D & G 9) J & M

Hats off to Mother

BY: ANGELA LANYON

All her life, Rose has failed to look good in a hat...

Maureen said: "I must say you are making an effort." She didn't actually add 'for once' but Rose, standing in front of the mirror, sensed the unspoken comment. She hardly recognised herself; the blue dress and jacket looked strange – casual shirts and trousers were more her line.

"Aren't you going to do something with your hair?" Maureen asked.

"In a minute." Rose tried not to snap. She rifled through her bag for a comb, then tipped the contents on to the bed. Lipsticks, tissues and a mascara rolled across the quilt. She heard Maureen's indrawn breath as she attacked her mane of blonde hair. The comb had two teeth missing – Maureen was sure to notice that.

"I don't believe it!" Maureen was peering into the carrier bag beside the dressing table. "You've got a hat! Whatever possessed you?"

Rose didn't know what had possessed her. She'd never liked hats. Her earliest memory was of her mother putting a sun hat on her at the seaside. There she'd been, pretending to be a mermaid singing on a rock, when two hands descended out of nowhere and she felt she'd been snuffed out like a candle. Rose still recalled her deep sense of affront that anyone should cover her golden curls.

School was the worst. In those far-off days girls' uniforms included hats. Nasty felt hats, shaped like pudding basins with scratchy elastic under the chin.

"Rose Burton, where is your hat?" was the cry forever on the lips of any member of staff who spotted her coming through the gates, bareheaded. Sometimes the hat was squashed in her satchel, sometimes hanging carelessly down her back.

"Young ladies attending St Hilary's wear hats in the street," the head mistress informed her sternly. Detention made no difference and neither did exclusion from hockey. Rose hadn't cared. She

'Young ladies wear hats in the street'

preferred to read or paint.

"Really, darling," her mother said sadly after the third letter from the school, "Maureen always gets good conduct marks, I do think you might make an effort."

"But I DO work!" Rose protested. And she did. There was never any complaint about the effort she put into lessons – only about her appearance.

"Hats are stupid," she declared, "and the school hat makes me look hideous. Anyway, wearing a hat won't make any difference when I leave school."

Her mother sighed again. "Well, darling, just try, will you? To please me."

Martyr-like, Rose set off the following morning. It was summer so she wore a straw boater with a blue and green band – fastened with the inevitable elastic. The day was hot. Rose loosened the hat. Draught from a passing van caught it, and sucked it under the wheels. The tyre marks made an interesting pattern but it was too squashed to wear.

When Rose was in the sixth form, she went on a school trip to France. The girls all wore attractive new berets but 20 minutes out of Dover and Rose's fell into the Channel as she leaned over the rail to look at the white cliffs.

"Oh, Rose!" exclaimed her mother in despair when she heard the tale. Despair turned to desperation when Rose was Maureen's bridesmaid. The wedding photographs were charming, except that Rose's wide-brimmed lilac hat had somehow fallen off and been sat on by a guest.

"I can't help my hair," Rose had once said to her mother. By then she was a rising star in the field of interior design with her own casual style of dress. "I suppose you'd rather I kept my crowning glory hidden. Anyway, what is it about hats?"

"I just think they finish off an outfit," her mother, who was in her 60s and still wore a hat although they were no longer fashionable, explained. "Maureen always manages to look smart even with three children to look after."

Rose tried not to sound resentful when she

'Maureen's always done the right thing...'

replied. "Maureen's always done the right thing, hasn't she?" I suppose you'd think more of me if I wore a hat and had a proper marriage licence instead of living with Tom."

Rose was successful enough to buy any number of expensive outfits and smart hats but when she spent so much time going up and down ladders and clambering about partly refurbished houses there wasn't much point. When she did wear a hat it was a safety helmet.

That conversation had been just a fortnight ago, the last time she had seen her mother. She had taken Rose's hand and laughed: "I love you just the same, with or without a hat."

Rose wondered now if she'd meant it.

She smoothed her skirt and her sister's eyes met hers in the mirror. Maureen passed her the carrier bag and Rose took out the hat. It was blue with blue and green ribbons, rather like the band on her school hat. Blue for the sky and green for the grass...

The hat had a wide brim and two feathers on one side. Instead of elastic to keep it in place, there was an elegant hatpin. She skewered it carefully through her hair. This time the hat was going to stay put.

Tom squeezed her fingers as they stood by the graveside. The coffin seemed small and lonely as it was lowered into the earth. It was a calm summer's day, then from nowhere came a gust of wind, lifting Rose's hat and spinning it over the wall. As she watched it disappear, Rose was sure she heard her mother's ghostly laugh.

June 2012

Friday
1

Saturday
2

Sunday
3

Monday
4
Spring Bank Holiday

Tuesday
5
Diamond Jubilee of Queen Elizabeth II

Wednesday
6

Thursday
7

Friday
8

Saturday
9

Sunday
10

Monday
11

Tuesday
12

Wednesday
13

Thursday
14
Trooping the Colour

Friday
15

Saturday
16

Sunday
17
Fathers' Day

Monday
18

Tuesday
19

Wednesday
20

Thursday
21
Longest Day (Summer Solstice)

Friday
22

Saturday **23**	**Wednesday** **27**
Sunday **24**	**Thursday** **28**
Monday **25** *Wimbledon tennis begins*	**Friday** **29**
Tuesday **26**	**Saturday** **30**

PIC: ISTOCKPHOTO

Poem of
the month

The June bride

I sit at the other end of the room
Wond'ring if he'll be your true bridegroom.
Your eyes look troubled, are you sure
You'll love him rich and love him poor?

What are you thinking, my pretty miss?
Do you recall our very first kiss?
We go back a long way, as you well know.
Don't you remember, I was your first beau?

So suave and sleek you are today,
Yet used to giggle and shriek at play.
Your heels are so high and your nails so long,
Yet your voice was loudest when we sang our song.

Your hair, now groomed to perfection,
I remember flying in every direction.
You are smiling, but are your eyes sad?
I need to know the truth because I'm your dad.

Mrs Pat Berkshire, Newcastle-upon-Tyne

My Teenage Years
Finally - the facts!

In the Fifties I went to a grammar school some ten miles away from the approved school where my father was an instructor. There was a limited bus service between my village and the town so I only mixed with boys of my own age during term time. It was a boys' school and it was against the rules to speak to girls in the street on pain of detention.

There was no sex education at the school but my father gave me a book to read supplied by the vicar. This was supposed to make things clear but I had no idea what it was about – it seemed to be all about white horses. Without any opportunity to chat to other teenagers, I remained in ignorance.

Aged 19, I gained a place at teachers' training college. Although there were male and

Victor (far left, middle row) with his new college mates

female students, we were housed in single-sex accommodation situated on each side of the main path through the college. The path was christened The Great Divide and the rule was that you had to be on your own side of it between 10pm and mid-day.

From discussions in the all-male common room, I finally caught up with the information that these days is taught to primary school pupils. Of course, The Great Divide was a challenge to all the students and, having had little opportunity to challenge rules when I was younger, I took every chance to break this rule, and prided myself on never being caught!

Victor Flute, Sudbury, Suffolk

Bird of the week

PIC: ISTOCK

Cuckoo

Traditionally, summer has begun when you hear the first Cuckoo. They arrive from central and southern Africa in April and leave again in July, so now is the best time to catch a glimpse. The Cuckoo is a brood parasite, which means it doesn't take any part in raising its young, laying its egg in the nest of another species like a Meadow Pipit or Dunnock. In order to fool the host, it changes the colour of its eggs to match the species it has chosen.
From Bird Watching magazine (www.birdwatching.co.uk)

Bright ideas

Cleaning a blender can be quite dangerous, especially getting dirt off the sharp blades. For a safer way half–fill it with warm water and a squeeze of washing up liquid, cover and turn on for a few seconds. Pour out and rinse and your blender should be spotless.

I wish I'd said that

"Wrinkles are hereditary. Parents get them from their children." **Doris Day reflects on the joys of being a parent.**

Only in Britain
Fun with a sting
Believe or not, us Brits hold the World Stinging Nettle Contest, which takes place in Marshwood, Dorset traditionally on the second Saturday in June. Contestants face one hour of eating this feisty plant. Rules are strict though and competitors are not permitted to bring their own nettles!

Our Tune
Love's Old Sweet Song – James Lyman Malloy and J Clifton Bingham
When we were children my Grandmother lived with us, and she always sang as she went about doing the housework. When she made the beds she sang 'Love's Old Sweet Song'. My sister and I called this "Nanny's Bed Song". It brings back happy memories of a lovely lady.   **Mrs E Ewing, Liverpool**

Photo I can't throw away

As a child my summer holidays were always spent in Cornwall on the North Coast. I got the surfing bug in my teenage years and here I am ready to go surfing, aged 18. I now live in Cornwall and, at the age of 66, still love to go surfing all year round. Last year I entered the World Belly Boarding Championships for the first time, and to my amazement I won the over-60s competition.

Christine Davies, Wadebridge, Cornwall

Recipe of the week

Melting Mushrooms with Eggs and Ham
Serves 2
Preparation time: 5 minutes
Cooking time: 8–10 minutes

◆ 4 large flat mushrooms, peeled
◆ 1 tbsp olive oil
◆ 4 medium eggs
◆ 2 slices thick-cut ham
◆ 50g (2 oz) double Gloucester cheese, grated

1 Preheat the grill to a medium heat and place the mushrooms on a baking tray. Drizzle with the oil and season well. Grill for 5 minutes, or until the mushrooms have softened slightly, turning once half way through cooking.
2 Meanwhile, poach the eggs in a saucepan of boiling water for 2–3 minutes, or until just set.
3 Place the mushrooms stalk side up on the baking tray, top with the ham, then the poached egg. Sprinkle over the cheese and grill for a further 2 minutes, or until the cheese is bubbling and golden. Serve immediately alongside a toasted wholegrain muffin and baked beans.
© Wholegrain Goodness, www.wholegraingoodness.com

My Teenage Years
Happy hols - hoeing!

Kathy (left) with Irene in 1946

One of my happiest memories was a holiday in 1946 with my friend Irene. We couldn't afford a week away but when we saw a poster saying 'Lend a Hand on the Land', we opted for a working holiday.

It cost the princely sum of £1 8s and was all arranged through the Ministry of Agriculture and Fisheries. We were given the choice of several counties and chose Oxfordshire. With the approval of our parents we went off to a small village called Forest Hill.

As we waited at Oxford station for our transport, we made friends with Joan and Kay from London who were going to the same place. When we arrived at the small army camp, we were allocated a wooden hut that slept four. We collected our matresses and caused great amusement when we asked for a key to the hut!

After two days spent hoeing cabbages, the rest of the week was ours. The weather was glorious. In the evening everyone, young and old, socialised. Joan played the piano so we all had 'a knees-up', as the Londoners called it.

One day, we had the chance of transport into Oxford. We walked round a church and in the college grounds. We decided to thumb a lift back. A man in a large, open-topped car stopped for us. He was interested in our holiday and dropped us at the camp. Not many ordinary people owned a car like that back then and I have often wondered who he was.

Kathy Eaton, Burton-on-Trent

Bird of the week

Herring Gull
PIC: ISTOCK

There are more than half a dozen different types of gulls commonly seen in the UK, and more that are rarer, but they are some of the hardest birds to tell apart so we tend to call them collectively 'seagulls'. Among the species we see are Black-headed Gulls, Great and Lesser Black-backed Gulls, and Kittiwakes, but the ones that congregate at the seaside to swoop down and steal our chips are probably Herring Gulls, those most opportunistic of gulls that also haunt landfill sites.
From Bird Watching magazine (www.birdwatching.co.uk)

Bright ideas

When you only need a couple of slices of bacon and have no immediate use for the rest of the pack, roll up slices into individual spirals and lay on a baking tray in the freezer until just frozen, or for 2-3 hours. Then pop into a freezer bag and use when needed.

I wish I'd said that

"My mother used to say the only reason men are alive is for lawn care and vehicle maintenance." **Comedian Tim Allen was given some sound advice from his mother.**

Only in Britain

Man versus Horse Marathon

Every June, in Llanwrytd Wells in Wales, man and horse battle it out over a 22 mile course. The event has been running since 1980, but it wasn't until 2004 that a man beat the horse competitors. Of course, horses do have the advantage of four legs instead of two!

Our Tune

My Heart Stood Still The First Time I Saw You – Rod Stewart

17 years old at St Mark's Youth Club in Battersea. Peter brought his brother, Geoff, who was also 17. That was it – I saw him and fell in love. It was weeks before he walked me home, and that first kiss was so wonderful. We married when we were 23.

Jean Casbolt, Honiton, Devon

Photo I can't throw away

This is a photograph of my Father taken in 1894 when he was a baby, with his parents who were 19 and 21 at the time. They lived in Marylebone, London, and had 13 children, but sadly only four of them lived to adulthood. My Father served in the Royal Horse Artillery in the First World War, and lived to be 89.

Mrs Knibbs, Buckingham

Recipe of the week

Mint Chocolate Cupcakes

Makes: 6–8
Preparation time: 20 minutes (plus 1 hour cooling)
Cooking time: 20 minutes

◆ 100g plain flour
◆ 25g cocoa powder
◆ 150g caster sugar
◆ 1½ tsp baking powder
◆ 50g salted butter, softened
◆ 100ml (4 fl oz) whole milk
◆ 1 medium egg
◆ 1 tsp vanilla extract
For the icing:
◆ 50g unsalted butter, softened
◆ 300g icing sugar
◆ 2–3 drops of peppermint extract
◆ 2–3 drops of green food colouring
◆ 6–8 chocolate mint squares, for decoration

1 Preheat the oven to 170°C/325°F/Gas Mark 3. Mix the dry ingredients and softened butter in a mixing bowl until it resembles breadcrumbs.
2 Mix the wet ingredients together, separately. Then pour half this mixture into the dry ingredients and mix until smooth. Repeat and stir gently until a smooth batter is formed.
3 Fill a muffin tin with cupcake cases (this amount makes between 6–8 cupcakes). Fill the cases half full with the batter and bake for 20 minutes, or until the tops are firm and springy and a skewer comes out clean when inserted. Leave to cool for five minutes before removing from the tin and cooling completely on a wire rack.
4 Meanwhile, make the icing by creaming the butter until light and fluffy. Then gradually add the icing sugar to form a smooth butter cream. You could add a little milk to help it cream. Then add the peppermint and food colouring and mix well. Chill until needed.
5 Before serving, pipe with a wide fluted nozzle or spoon the icing onto the cakes and top with mint thins.
© Nielsen-Massey Vanillas, www.nielsenmassey.com

My Teenage Years
Biba Babe

My memories of being a teenager in the Seventies are coloured by make-up – lots of it! When I was 13, looking in the mirror was my favourite pastime. The question most frequently on my mind was, 'How do I look?' And make-up was essential to getting that look just right.

I would spend hours reading the beauty pages of all the magazines to discover the latest products and more happy hours considering what to buy. Then I would spend ages scouring the make-up counters in our local high street shops, trying to decide whether this week's precious bit of pocket money would go on a lilac shimmery eye-shadow or a coral lipstick, pale blue nail varnish or a new mascara. My greatest pleasure was to visit the Biba counter in a shop that was on my way home from school. I'd smear a sample on my hand and contemplate it, telling myself how sophisticated I was, shopping in Biba (except I wasn't actually shopping, just fantasising about it).

Susan loved to browse in Biba and sample the make-up

When there was a school disco to get dolled-up for, I'd get together with my best friend and we would compare the contents of our make-up bags and try out new looks.

I'm still a big fan of make-up and wear it every day, but nothing can compare with the pleasure – and optimism – of those early experiments with glamour.

Susan Creed, Reading

Bird of the week

PIC: ISTOCK

House and Tree Sparrow

House Sparrows have been declining hugely in the UK but no one really knows why. Changes in farming are thought to have a bearing. Hygiene rules and being more efficient at storing grain and animal feed have cut down on ready food supplies and nesting places for these small birds. Tree Sparrows, which have brown on the top of their heads instead of grey, are also having a hard time, but in their case it is loss of hedgerows and woodlands that's probably to blame.
From Bird Watching magazine (www.birdwatching.co.uk)

Bright ideas

To save yourself the hassle of scrubbing your saucepans, if you regularly burn milk while boiling it, place a large glass marble in the bottom of the pan. As the milk boils, the motion of it in the pan will stir the milk as well as preventing it from scalding.

I wish I'd said that

"He is not only dull himself; he is the cause of dullness in others."
American statesman Samuel Johnson

Only in Britain
Well dressed
If you're lucky between the end of May and September you might stumble across some of the best-dressed wells in the country. The unusual tradition of well dressing still takes place in some areas of Derbyshire and Staffordshire and involves wells being dressed with pictures made from flowers and plants.

Our Tune
Give Me The Stars – Leni Lynn
On our first date, Eric and I saw the film 'Give Me The Stars'. Walking home, Eric pointed out the constellation Orion. He said they would be our stars, and represent this song. I never thought 66 years later we would still be putting stars on letters to each other.
Doreen Leighton, Leeds

Photo I can't throw away

This family photo was taken on holiday in Southend in about 1925 when I was eight. I am the boy at the front with my mother just behind – my father was killed just before the end of the First World War. The girl beside me was my cousin, with her parents behind. Top right is her elder brother with another uncle. I've been much further for holidays recently, having friends in Germany and New Zealand, and a sister-in-law in California.

Jack Savory, Kingston-upon-Thames, Surrey

Recipe of the week

Sweet Pepper Gazpacho
Serves: 4
Preparation time: 10 minutes
Cooking time: 30 minutes (plus 2 hours chilling)

◆ 2 red peppers
◆ 1/2 small red onion, chopped
◆ 700g ripe tomatoes, peeled and chopped
◆ 1/2 cucumber, chopped
◆ 2 cloves of garlic, crushed
◆ 200g breadcrumbs made from Ciabatta bread
◆ 4 tbsp olive oil (plus extra for brushing)
◆ 1 tsp white wine vinegar
◆ 600ml (1 pint) tomato Juice
◆ 300ml (12 fl oz) water
◆ 1 small handful fresh basil leaves

1 Preheat the oven to 200°C/400°F/Gas Mark 6. Halve and de-seed the red peppers, brush with oil and roast for about 30 minutes, or until soft. Leave to cool to room temperature.
2 Then place the peppers, onion, tomatoes, cucumber, garlic, breadcrumbs, olive oil and vinegar in a food processor and blend until smooth. Add the tomato juice, water, basil leaves and blend briefly to mix. Season to taste and put in the fridge to chill for a couple of hours at least.
3 Just before serving, garnish with ice cubes and the basil leaves. Serve with crusty Ciabatta bread.

◆ **Top tip:** You can make and chill this up to 3 days before you need it.
© Flour Advisory Bureau, www.fabflour.co.uk

My Teenage Years
Our radio days

The kitchen was where my family gathered to listen to the radio. Saturday morning was always Children's Favourites with wonderful songs like Sparky and the Magic Piano and Tubby the Tuba. On Sundays, we listened to comedies like The Clitheroe Kid while we ate our roast dinner.

My sister, Barbara, and I shared a bedroom and loved to listen to Radio Luxembourg when we were in bed. The Top 20 hit parade was interrupted by advertising jingles. The one I remember best was for Horace Batchelor's Infra-Draw method of winning the football pools in which he painstakingly spelt out his address of Keynsham, Bristol. Another regular advert reminded us that 'Friday night is Amami night'. Amami was a sticky setting lotion guaranteed to produce an abundance of waves in readiness for the weekend.

Our front room (or parlour as we called it then) housed our much-prized radiogram. Oh, the joy of stacking up the records on the spindle and

Linda strolls with a young relative and her Mum and Dad

watching them dropping down on to the turntable! The first record I bought was Frank Ifield singing I Remember You. Barbara's collection included Eve Boswell's Pickin' a Chicken with Me and the Everly Brothers singing Cathy's Clown.

In 1958 we got our first television. Among the programmes I liked were Junior Criss Cross Quiz and Double Your Money, a quiz game presented by Hughie Green. Contestants who reached the dizzy height of £32 had to go into a soundproof booth and answer questions against the clock to win the princely sum of £64.

Linda Burns, Stoke-on-Trent

Bird of the week

Pied Wagtail

PIC: ISTOCK

These are the supermarket car park and motorway services birds. Tiny, delicate, and black and white with long wagging tails, they seem to take their lives into their hands dashing around among parked cars looking for insects. In winter, Pied Wagtails can form huge roosts at night, especially in trees in town centres, where the birds huddle together for warmth. You can increase your chances of attracting a Pied Wagtail to your garden if you dig a pond, which will promote some of their favourite insects.
From Bird Watching magazine (www.birdwatching.co.uk)

Bright ideas

Make your non-stick cookware last longer by reusing the bubble wrap you get with parcels. Simply use it as a protective layer between pans when you come to storing them in the cupboard. This prevents the non-stick surface being scratched off by the bases of other pans.

I wish I'd said that

"Well at least he has finally found his true love... what a pity he can't marry himself."
Frank Sinatra lets loose on Robert Redford.

Only in Britain

That's charming

Yes, worm charming does exist and there's even an annual charming contest. Legend has it that a farmer's son once charmed 511 out of the ground in 30 minutes! The rules include no digging and after the event worms are to be released at night when the birds are roosting.

Our Tune

San Francisco (Be Sure To Wear Flowers In Your Hair) – Scott Mackenzie

In 1969 I left secondary school at the height of the hippy era. This song was playing as we were dismissed from the last assembly, and it suddenly dawned on me that this group of people I had seen every day for five years would never see each other again.

Pam Richardson, Tansor, Northants

Photo I can't throw away

It is only since both my parents have passed away that I regret not taking more photos of them. We have so few, and I dread to think what would happen if I lost them. This one was taken on their wedding day, June 25, 1958. They couldn't be married in a church because my father had been divorced, so it was a register office wedding.

Lena Walton, Tadworth, Surrey

Recipe of the week

Cranberry Summer Pudding

Serves: 6
Preparation time: 20 minutes
Chilling time: at least 2 hours (preferably overnight)

◆ 400g all-butter Madeira loaf
◆ 175g whole strawberries, hulled
◆ 150g fresh raspberries
◆ 3 small whole figs
◆ 125g blueberries
◆ 200g whole berries cranberry sauce
◆ 150ml (6 fl oz) lemon jelly, made with boiling water
◆ 150ml 6 fl oz) double cream
◆ Extra berries, double cream and fresh mint leaves, to serve

1 Line a 1.3 litre (2¼ pint) pudding basin with cling-film. Cut the Madeira cake into 11 thin slices and use 9 to line the base and sides of the basin overlapping the slices slightly. Trim the protruding ends of the cake to fit, and reserve the trimmings.
2 In a separate bowl, mix the fruit together with the cranberry sauce and then pack tightly into the cake lined pudding basin. Pour the jelly into the double cream and stir well. Gradually pour over the fruit, allowing the mixture to sink into the fruit before pouring again. Arrange the remaining Madeira cake slices over the top of the fruit along with the reserved trimmings. Chill for at least 2 hours or preferably overnight if you have time, or until just set.
3 Carefully turn out onto a plate just before serving and remove the cling-film. Decorate with the fresh berries and mint leaves. Serve in wedges with extra-thick double cream.
© Ocean Spray, www.oceanspray.co.uk

Time for fun

This pretty project would make a lovely gift or is a great project to make with your grandchildren

Takes 3 hours

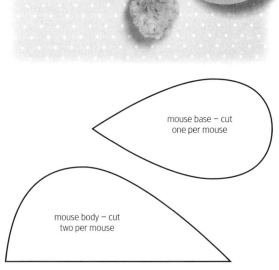

You will need:

Fabrics in three contrasting colours and patterns
Felt in white and grey
1m cord
1 small black button
4 small black beads
Double sided tape
Toy filling

2 grey pom-poms (around $2^{1}/_{2}$ inch)
Embroidery thread in black, pink and grey-blue
Needle
PVA glue
Sheets of heavy weight card
Scissors

◆ **Make sure you let your clock dry completely before hanging.**

Clock

1 Cut two identical pieces of card for the front and back of the clock (these should be plant pot shaped ie wider at the top). From the card also cut two rectangle side panels the same height as the front. Cover with fabric securing with double-sided tape. Next, cut out two smaller rectangles the same width as the sides to create a roof. Cover in the same way with a different fabric, but covering the undersides too as these will be visible.

2 Cut a circle of white felt and attach to the front panel using large stitches of the grey-blue thread. Add the clock hands and a small button in the centre using black thread. Stitch all the panels together using the grey-blue thread and large stitches picking up the fabric only (don't stitch through the card). After stitching the two roof panels together, attach these to the clock body with a bead of glue and secure temporarily with pins. Leave to dry thoroughly before removing pins.

3 Cut a 70cm length of cord and stitch a pom-pom to each end. Fold the cord and sit the fold in a blob of glue on the inside centre of the back panel. Leave to dry flat.

Mouse

4 Using the template and grey felt cut enough pieces to make two mice. Sew the edges with a plain or blanket stitch using three strands of the pink embroidery thread. Don't forget to add the tail (knot on the inside of the body to secure) and leave a small opening to allow for stuffing.

mouse base – cut one per mouse

mouse body – cut two per mouse

5 Stitch both mice closed, then add two small fabric ears, two beads for eyes and black thread whiskers. Complete by stitching the mice to the clock using a strand of the blue-grey thread.

For more great craft projects and all your crafting supplies call 01202 596100 or visit www.hobbycraft.co.uk.

Quiz of the month

Test your knowledge of light entertainment shows. If you get stuck the answers are below.

When did these two famous faces air as a comedy duo?

1 What was Eric Morecambe's real name?

2 Which comedian from Dudley, West Midlands won New Faces several times?

3 Who hosted Opportunity Knocks between 1987 and 1990?

4 The first series of The Two Ronnies was broadcast in which year?

5 Which member of Monty Python's Flying Circus was American?

6 Who was Tony Hancock's side-kick in Hancock's Half Hour?

7 Who presented Kaleidoscope?

8 Name the double act that present the current Saturday night television programme Push The Button?

9 Morecambe and Wise poked fun at many celebrities. There was one in particular, who came in for a lot of criticism. Who was it?

10 Who was the original presenter of New Faces?

11 When was the first episode of Hancock's Half Hour broadcast?

12 Which famous magician made his television debut on Opportunity Knocks (he came second)?

13 Name any of the regular hosts of Sunday Night at the London Palladium – extra credit if you can remember them all.

14 What was the long-running catchphrase of diminutive magician Paul Daniels?

15 Can you name the variety show hosted by comedian Colin Crompton, that was set in a fictional Working Men's Club?

ANSWERS: 1) John Eric Bartholomew, 2) Lenny Henry, 3) Bob Monkhouse, 4) 1971, 5) Terry Gilliam, 6) Sid James, 7) McDonald Hobley, 8) Ant and Dec, 9) Des O'Connor, 10) Derek Hobson, 11) 1954, 12) Paul Daniels, 13) Tommy Trinder, Bruce Forsyth, Norman Vaughan, Jimmy Tarbuck and Jim Dale, 14) "You'll like this…not a lot, but you'll like it", 15) The Wheeltappers and Shunters Social Club

Sunday

1

Monday

2

Tuesday

3

Wednesday

4

American Independence Day

Thursday

5

Friday

6

Saturday

7

Sunday

8

Monday

9

Tuesday

10

Wednesday

11

Thursday

12

Battle of the Boyne
(Bank Holiday Northern Ireland)

Friday

13

Saturday

14

Sunday

15

St Swithun's Day

Monday

16

Tuesday

17

Wednesday

18

Thursday

19

Friday

20

Saturday

21

Sunday

22

Monday **23**	Saturday **28**
Tuesday **24**	Sunday **29**
Wednesday **25**	Monday **30**
Thursday **26**	Tuesday **31**
Friday **27** *London Olympics opening ceremony*	

PIC: ISTOCKPHOTO

Poem of the month

Summer tranquillity

Innocent, unwary,
Fledglings ponder their new world.
The cat lurks in the long grass,
Infinitely patient…
In ceaseless quest
Bees seek the sweetest flowers.
Dragonflies zig-zag dazzlingly
On iridescent wings.
A fragrant scent wafts
From a full-blown rose.
The breeze ruffles the leaves,
Whispering, quivering.
A smouldering hint of barbecue
Is carried on the air.
Agreeably indolent,
I lie drowsing in my hammock.
Then strident, jarring,
A mower scythes the peace!
My tranquillity is over;
It is fading, it has gone.
Brenda Edwards, Coleford, Glos

July 2 - 8

My Teenage Years
Nylon heaven

When I left school and started work at the age of 14, I had to start wearing a suspender belt and stockings. In those days, there were three types of stockings to choose from. Lisle stockings were made of cotton, almost as thick as wool, and they wrinkled like Nora Batty's in Last of the Summer Wine. Pure silk stockings were expensive and so fine that they did not last very long. Artificial silk stockings were more affordable but I hated wearing them because they felt very tight around your legs.

A friend who worked in Marshall & Snelgrove's department store told me about stockings made from a new material called nylon that was as fine as silk but much more durable. They cost 9s 11d.

Out of my weekly wage of 22s 6d, I gave my mother £1 which left me with 2s 6d pocket money – so there was no way I could afford to buy a pair of nylons. But, unbeknown to me, my mother bought me a pair as a surprise present.

They were a joy to wear. They were fully

Marie can never forget her first pair of nylons

fashioned with a shaped heel and a seam up the back that had to be kept straight. And they lasted for months and months. It was not long before nylons became widely available and cheaper to buy but I never had any as good as that first pair which I wore so proudly.

Marie Jaques, Scarborough

Bird of the week

PIC: ISTOCK

Skylark

A tiny speck high up in a sunny blue sky, singing its heart out, is a cherished sight and sound of a British summer. Skylarks live in open country, making their nests in small depressions in grasslands and in among young cereal crops. The songs we hear are proclamations of a male's territory. They rise up almost vertically, sometimes as high as 1,000 feet and hover for many minutes, even up to an hour, before parachuting back down to the ground.
From Bird Watching magazine (www.birdwatching.co.uk)

Bright ideas

If you have a teething grandchild, ease their sore gums by giving them a piece of frozen banana to munch on instead of the usual teething ring. It soothes pain and they will be getting some essential vitamins at the same time.

I wish I'd said that

"Whatever kind of look you were going for, you missed."

Only in Britain

Bog snorkelling

Bog snorkelling is said to have been born in Wales in the Seventies and this mucky sport has grown into an annual event. Held in August, bog snorkelling involves contestants snorkelling, complete with flippers, through peat bogs without using recognised swimming strokes. Held in Llanwrtyd Wells in Wales.

Our Tune

It's Not Unusual – Tom Jones

Back in the Sixties I had a portable Dansette record player. One family holiday, we were having a great time listening to records. Then I put Tom Jones on. He sang in slow motion – the heat had melted my record! I still smile now thinking of those long summer days.

Margaret Dinsdale, Newcastle-upon-Tyne

Photo I can't throw away

My best holidays were in Britain in the Sixties. I could hardly wait for July to come when my family and I would pack up Bessie, our car, and set off for our annual holiday in St Ives, Cornwall. My favourite day was always the one we spent at the beach. We'd gather our buckets and spades, and spend the day building sandcastles, watching the boats in the harbour and paddling in the sea. Happy days.

Dale Gibson, Watford, Hertfordshire

Recipe of the week

Sweet Chilli and Herb Burgers

Serves: 4
Preparation time: 15 minutes (plus 20 minutes chilling time)
Cooking time: 8-10 minutes

- ◆ 450g lamb or beef mince
- ◆ 1 small onion, peeled and grated
- ◆ 1 large garlic clove, peeled and finely crushed
- ◆ 2 tbsp fresh flat-leaf parsley, finely chopped
- ◆ 1 tbsp fresh mint, finely chopped
- ◆ 3 tbsp sweet chilli dipping sauce

For the relish:
- ◆ 4 small cooked beetroot (not in vinegar), finely chopped
- ◆ 4 tbsp low-fat crème fraîche or Greek yogurt
- ◆ 2 tbsp fresh mint, roughly chopped

1 In a large bowl mix all the burger ingredients together until well blended. Then, using slightly damp hands, shape the mixture into four 10cm (4 inch) burgers. Cover and chill for 20 minutes.
2 Meanwhile, preheat the grill to medium and cook the burgers for 8-10 minutes, turning occasionally, until they are thoroughly cooked and any meat juices run clear.
3 While they are cooking, prepare the relish by placing all the ingredients into a small bowl and mix gently. Serve the burgers topped with a spoonful of the relish in toasted bread rolls of your choice.

◆ **Top tip:** For the best-tasting burgers, don't use a reduced fat mince. With the relish, avoid beetroot stains on the hands by wearing disposable plastic gloves when preparing it.
© www.simplybeefandlamb.co.uk

My Teenage Years
Brand new roller skates

In July 1959 I was about to take the giant step into the big wide world after leaving King John School in Benfleet. I pleaded with my parents to allow me to have the summer off before starting work. They agreed and I spent those hot, sunny months doing what I enjoyed most – swimming in Westcliff-on-Sea open air pool and roller-skating on the rink on Southend pier.

For my fifteenth birthday in August, my parents gave me a pair of white roller-skating boots which I cherished. I wore them when we played Two Down and One Pushing (where two skaters crouch down, holding on to each other, and a third person pushed them along). The winners were the ones who went the longest without collapsing.

In September, I started my first job on the beauty counter of the chemist, Longthornes. My wage was £3 a week; £1 of that went on bus fares and £1 10s to my mum, leaving me with 10s to live on. It was while I was at work that I heard one of the customers telling another shop assistant that Southend pier had burned down. I felt shattered and wept that evening.

My heart was set on a job in London and I was delighted when I was taken on as a junior clerk with an insurance company in the City. My dad helped with my first month's train fare which I duly repaid out of my first month's salary.   **Bobbie Jones, Benfleet, Essex**

Bobbie in 1968

Bird of the week

PIC: ISTOCK

Bullfinch

One of the most beautiful birds to visit our gardens, Bullfinches are not hugely popular with gardeners because of their habit of eating the young flower buds on fruit trees. The male is the gaudier bird with a bright red breast and cheeks, grey back and black cap. Our resident birds tend to be quite shy, but in winter they're joined by other Bullfinches from northern Europe that are much more ready to show themselves at the top of a hedge.
From Bird Watching magazine (www.birdwatching.co.uk)

Bright ideas

To keep freshly-baked cookies and brownies softer for longer, place a slice of bread in the storage container with them. The moisture from the bread keeps them soft and retains that 'just-baked' flavour. If the bread dries out, simply replace it with another slice until all the cookies have been scoffed.

I wish I'd said that

"Keep talking, someday you'll say something intelligent!"

Only in Britain

I had a little hobby horse

Hobby horses have links in England as far back as the 16th century and have delighted children nationwide ever since. So, it shouldn't be much of a surprise that there are dedicated events nationwide, with parades, music, dancing and, of course, lots of hobby horses!

Our Tune

Putting On The Style – Lonnie Donegan

When I came to England in 1957 to marry my husband, I couldn't speak much English. When we saw the vicar, he asked me: "What hymn would you like?" I just said 'Putting On The Style' as it was the song of the day, much to the amusement of everyone!

Christina Mallett, Bury St Edmunds

Photo I can't throw away

This photograph is of my Mum and Dad, my brother and me in 1932. I had whooping cough, so my parents took me to the seaside. We went out on a boat and I was very sick. Then we went to the photographer to have this family picture taken. I am 81 now and sadly the only one of the family left, but I will never forget that day, and it certainly cured my whooping cough.

Doris Taylor, Newcastle-upon-Tyne

Recipe of the week

Peach Pie with Ginger and Honey

Serves: 6-8
Preparation time: 20 minutes
Cooking time: 40 minutes

For the pastry:
- 300g plain flour
- 2 tbsp caster sugar
- 100g butter, melted
- 1 egg

For the filling:
- 425g can of sliced peaches in natural juice, drained
- 200g golden marzipan, coarsely grated
- 3 eggs
- 300ml (12 fl oz) Oatly Enriched or Organic oat drink
- 1 tbsp fresh ginger, grated
- 3 tbsp runny honey

To serve:
- Runny honey and custard or vanilla ice cream

1 Heat the oven to 200°C/400°F/Gas Mark 6. Put the flour, sugar, salt and melted butter into a food processor and pulse until blended. Then add the eggs and mix into a smooth dough.
2 On a lightly floured surface, roll the dough out to fit into a loose-bottomed 23 cm (9 inch) circular pie dish. Prick the base and line with foil, then bake for 10 minutes. Remove the foil and bake for a further 5 minutes.
3 In a separate bowl, mix together the marzipan, egg, Oatly oat drink, grated ginger and honey. Pour into the pastry case and arrange the peach slices on top.
4 Reduce the oven temperature to 180°C/350°F/ Gas Mark 4 and bake for 25 minutes, or until the filling is set.
5 Drizzle over a little extra honey and serve immediately or leave to cool completely.
© Oatly, www.oatly.co.uk

My Teenage Years
Fashion victim

In 1973 I was working at Daniel Doncaster's steelworks in Sheffield. A few months before my eighteenth birthday I caught the bus that took me to the top of Bamforth Street from where I walked down to the works. It was raining heavily so I was wearing my long zip-up leather boots with three-inch platform soles and even higher heels.

As the bus slowed to a halt, I jumped off and landed awkwardly in a grating. I felt a terrific pain in my ankle and two women helped me to walk to Doncaster's where they insisted I went to the medical room. The nurse said my ankle was badly sprained; she strapped it up and told me to come back in a week. Luckily, my job was in an office so I was able to sit down and rest it.

A few days later, I was going out to the Top Rank disco. I unstrapped my ankle and set off in another pair of three-inch platform shoes. After four hours of dancing energetically to the glam rock records of the day, I began to regret my decision. I limped out

A sprained ankle didn't put Elaine off platform heels

and got a taxi home where Mam strapped my ankle back up.

I never went back to see the nurse as I was frightened of getting a telling off (I was very shy in those days). Now that I am 55, I still have trouble with that ankle – but we all think we know best when we're young, don't we?

Elaine Dale, Sowerby Bridge, W Yorkshire

Bird of the week

PIC: ISTOCK

Goldfinch

These birds have to be some of the most colourful to come to our gardens, with their red face masks and yellow wing patches in among their buff, cream and white plumage. They have become well-known to many garden birdwatchers of late because of their liking for nyjer, the tiny black seeds of an African herb, that are highly nutritious despite their size. In the wild, Goldfinches enjoy thistle and teasel seeds, their long, fine beaks helping them to extract them efficiently from the plants.
From Bird Watching magazine (www.birdwatching.co.uk)

Bright ideas

Hot hands and a hot kitchen can mean disaster for pastry, which needs to be kept as chilled as possible when handling. Remedy this by freezing your rolling pin for 20 minutes before use. It'll mean less contact with warm hands and surroundings and result in a tastier pie – hopefully!

I wish I'd said that

Try this corker from Humphrey Bogart in the film Casablanca (1942):
Peter Lorre as Ugarte: "You despise me, don't you?'
Humphrey Bogart as Rick: "If I gave you any thought, I probably would."

Only in Britain

Ready, steady, slow

The World Snail Racing Championships is not to be missed, although entertainment can be a bit slow! This batty event takes place annually in Congham, Norfolk, where it has been hosted for 25 years. More than 200 snails battle it out for the title and a tankard stuffed with lettuce.

Our Tune

Begin the Beguine – Cole Porter

In 1941 I was in the WAAF, and went to a local soldiers' camp concert. There I met Danny. Next night we met on Clifton suspension bridge, where we sang and danced to this tune. Every chance we got we met at the bridge, and continued our song and dance.

P Smailes, Ryton, Tyne and Wear

Photo I can't throw away

This picture was taken on a Box Brownie camera. It is of my wife Valerie and myself making a sandcastle on the sands at Barry Island, South Wales in 1936, when I was four years old and Valerie was three. We were next-door-neighbours until her family moved away to Bristol, but we kept in contact and, 76 years later, have a daughter, a son and four grandchildren. I keep this photograph in my wallet at all times.

Clive Brimfield, Newbridge, Gwent

Recipe of the week

Bacon and Mushroom Kebabs

Serves: 4-6
Preparation time: 10 minutes (plus10 minutes marinating time)
Cooking time: 8-10 minutes

- ◆ 1 tbsp olive oil
- ◆ 1 tbsp wholegrain mustard
- ◆ 1 tbsp clear honey
- ◆ 250g pack whole chestnut mushrooms
- ◆ 1 large yellow pepper, deseeded and cut into big chunks
- ◆ 6 rashers of smoked streaky bacon
- ◆ Hot-dog rolls and salad, to serve

1 Soak 4-6 bamboo skewers in warm water, to prevent them burning while cooking. In a large bowl, mix together the oil, mustard and honey with a little salt and plenty of ground black pepper. Add the mushrooms and pepper and toss well to coat. Leave to marinate for 10 minutes.
2 Meanwhile, preheat the grill to hot, or barbecue. Use the back of a knife to stretch each rasher of bacon, then cut each rasher in half. Roll up each half to make a bacon roll.
3 Thread a piece of pepper, mushroom and then a bacon roll onto a skewer. Repeat until all the ingredients are used up and brush any remaining marinade over the kebabs.
4 Barbecue, or grill for about 10 minutes, turning the kebabs so that they are golden brown on all sides. Remove the skewers, place in toasted hot-dog rolls and serve immediately with salad leaves.
© The Mushroom Bureau, www.mushroomsmakesense.com

My Teenage Years
Grounded!

At the age of 16, my deadline for getting home was 10pm so I knew when I missed my usual bus that I was in dead trouble. My Dad was going to kill me! But, as I looked at my watch, I had an idea. If I turned the hands back to ten past nine, I could pretend that my watch wasn't working. All I had to do was act innocent…

Both Mom and Dad were waiting to pounce when I opened the kitchen door. "What time do you call this?" They looked relieved to see me and I felt guilty for worrying them.

"What do you mean?" Swallowing hard, I held out my wrist. "I'm early!"

My parents weren't fooled for a second and I was told in no uncertain terms that after this deception I could forget about going to the dance hall the following night. All the next day, I sat miserably in our living room, pretending to do my homework. My eyes kept going to the half-crown, my pocket money, which Mom had placed, as usual, on the mantelpiece.

Carol's temptation to lie nearly back-fired on her fun

It would have paid for my bus fare, entrance to the dance and a bag of chips, if I hadn't been grounded for being a liar.

The hours passed agonisingly slowly until finally, at seven o'clock my dad took a look at my long face and sighed: "Go on then – off to your rock 'n' roll. But let this be a lesson to you, young lady!"

To this day, I can remember how happy I felt!

Carol Hathorne, Willenahll

Bird of the week

PIC: ISTOCK

Collared Dove

Only arriving in this country in 1955, the Collared Dove has since established that our habitat suits them very well. They have expanded massively to become one of our most common birds, particularly around farms and gardens. The birds don't migrate over large distances like many others, but they do colonise very efficiently, so the young of a pair will move mainly westward away from their parents to establish a new territory and their young will move westwards again, and so on.
From Bird Watching magazine (www.birdwatching.co.uk)

Bright ideas

Sometimes a pair of sharp scissors are better than a knife. Ideal for cutting up dried fruits for cake recipes. They also work wonders on snipping up bacon or cooked pizzas just before serving. It also means less washing up as you don't need a chopping board.

I wish I'd said that

"Do you have to leave so soon? I was about to poison the tea."

Only in Britain

Wedded bliss

According to superstition the day you wed says a lot about your marriage's outcome. The saying goes: Monday for health, Tuesday for wealth, Wednesday best of all, Thursday for losses, Friday for crosses, Saturday for no luck at all. Worrying, because Saturday is now the most common day to get hitched.

Our Tune

Spanish Eyes – Al Martino

This is my favourite song. When my husband was alive, no matter what we were doing or where we were, we got up and danced to it. Although he died 18 years ago, it still gives me pleasure as I think he is watching over me when it comes on.

P Campbell, Aldridge, West Midlands

Photo I can't throw away

This photograph of me, my late parents Hilda and Edwin, and my sister Margaret, taken in 1947 in Holt, Norfolk, is so nostalgic for me. I was nine years old, recovering from tuberculosis, and convalescing at The Children's Sanatorium, where I spent nine months. Holt was a long way from home and my parents saved up to be able to spend a week visiting me every day during my father's holiday from work – hence our happy faces.

Janet Lambert, Longfield, Kent

Recipe of the week

Tropical Fruit Pavlova

Serves: 8
Preparation time: 20 minutes
Cooking time: 2 hours (plus 1 hour cooling time)

◆ 200ml (8 fl oz) egg whites
◆ 250g caster sugar
◆ 200ml (8 fl oz) double cream
◆ 1 small ripe mango, peeled and pitted
◆ 1/2 ripe papaya, peeled and deseeded
◆ 1 kiwi fruit, peeled
◆ 100g strawberries

1 Preheat the oven to 140°C/275°F/Gas Mark 1. Line a baking sheet with non-stick baking parchment and draw a 251/2cm (10 inch) circle onto it.
2 In a large grease-free bowl and using a hand-held electric whisk, whip the egg whites until they form peaks. Gradually add the sugar, whisking well until stiff and glossy.
3 Spread the meringue onto the baking sheet in an even layer sticking to inside the marked out circle.
4 Bake for 2 hours, or until the meringue is dried out. Leave to cool completely.
5 Meanwhile, whip the cream until stiff and chill until needed. Thinly slice the mango, papaya and kiwi fruit and halve the strawberries and chill until needed.
6 Just before serving, spread the cream on top of the meringue and arrange the fruit on top. Serve immediately.

◆ **Top tip:** You can also use British berries instead of tropical fruit.
© Two Chicks Egg Whites, www.twochicks.co.uk

Summer Blooms

This simple Hydrangea flower arrangement proves you don't have to be a florist to create a stunning display for your home

You will need:

A fish bowl
(around 41cm/16inch high)
6 pink hydrangea
flower heads
A woven vine base or something
similar (optional)

1 Put a small amount of water in the fish bowl – the water should only be about 5cm (2inch) deep. Stick to hydrangeas for this display as they're one of the few flowers whose petals are course enough to tolerate sitting in water.

2 Cut the stems of three of the flower heads slightly shorter than the others and arrange them first placing the stems in the water.

3 Take the remaining three flower heads and carefully insert their slightly longer stems in between the bottom layer of flowers until the stems sit in the water. The lower layer of flower heads should help keep these uppermost blooms stable. Fluff out the hydrangea petals so they are not squashed.

4 Position your vine base around your bowl for effect.

Takes 30 minutes

◆ Help your display last longer by refreshing the water and re-cutting the stems.

Flower Arranging (£20), by Mark Welford and Stephen Wicks, published by DK, available from all good bookshops and online at www.dk.com.

Quiz of the month

The following children's television shows might jog a few memories.
See how many you can answer, if you get stuck the answers are below.

1 Can you name the five toys from Play School?

2 Which night of the week was Crackerjack on?

3 Can you name the three men, who hosted Screen Test over the 14 years it ran?

4 Which champion boxer was a co-presenter on Six Five Special?

5 What was the name of the first pet to appear on Blue Peter?

6 Who presented Juke Box Jury? Extra credit if you can get all three.

7 Who was the main presenter of Record Breakers?

8 In We Are the Champions, what was Ron Pickering well known for shouting at the end of each programme?

9 What does it mean when the Blue Peter flag is hoisted by a ship?

10 Which year was Top of the Pops first broadcast?

11 Name one of the original presenters for Play School.

12 Pete Murray was the male host of Six Five Special, but who was the female?

13 The Beatles were one of the first guests on the launch show of TOTPs, but which of their hits did the band play?

14 In Blue Peter, what did presenter John Noakes always say to his excitable dog?

15 In the final show of Screen Test, which children's television programme was the opposing team from?

16 Name the excitable young performer who hosted outside broadcasts on Swap Shop.

17 Which famous DJ hosted the very first Top of the Pops show?

PIC REXFEATURES

ANSWERS: 1) Jemima, Humpty, Big Ted, Little Ted or Hamble the Doll 2) Friday 3) Michael Rodd, Brian Trueman or Mark Curry 4) Freddie Mills 5) Petra 6) David Jacobs, Noel Edmonds, Jools Holland 7) Roy Castle 8) "Away Y Go" 9) It's about to leave on a journey 10) 1958 11) Virginia Stride or Gordon Rollings 12) Josephine Douglas 13) I Want To Hold Your Hand 14) "Get down Shep" 16) Grange Hill 17) Keith Chegwin 18) Jimmy Savile

Hello, handsome!

BY: JENNIFER KISSANE

Judith dreams of a holiday romance – but Jean disapproves!

Judith tried to ignore the fluttering in her stomach as she approached the bar. The barman gave her a warm smile and asked: "Same again?" His ocean-blue eyes gazed into hers as he awaited her response.

"Yes, please," she replied, returning the smile. She could feel Jean's glare burning holes into her back. In fact, Jean had spotted the dashing barman first. Judith tried to dismiss her guilt – after all Jean had a husband to go home to and she didn't. Rex had been dead five years now and she missed male company. It didn't seem like five years; she still rolled over some mornings and expected to find her sleeping husband beside her. She missed watching the rise and fall of his chest as he slept, and hearing the sound of his gentle breathing.

Ever since Rex had passed away Jean had made a point of accompanying her on an annual holiday. This year the destination had been the west coast of Ireland. Judith fell instantly in love with the rugged coastline and stony beaches. She found the bite of the sea breeze refreshing. Jean complained of the damp and the dreariness. "I knew we should have gone to Spain again!" she moaned. "This place is freezing!"

"There you go," the barman said, placing the drinks on the counter. Judith fumbled with her purse: "I just can't get used to this currency."

The barman laughed. "Here, let me help you." He leaned further over the counter. The smell of his aftershave made her tingle. He looked to be in his late thirties; his raven black hair peppered with grey. It reminded her of that actor that Jean cooed about when they'd been to the cinema the night before. Sometimes it amazed Judith that Jean's marriage had survived all these years – her gaze was always wandering.

She smiled secretly to herself as she remembered

Judith fell in love with the rugged coastline

what Rex used to say whenever he noticed her admiring a stranger. Nudging her playfully, he'd whisper: "Lucky I'm not the jealous type."

Judith couldn't help being flirtatious. Her late husband had been no George Clooney. His attraction lay in his gentle nature and quick wit. She was glad that her new fancy, with his chiselled good looks, was so different. She didn't want a substitute. If she were ever to love another she wanted to love them for different reasons. She doubted that anyone could ever reach her as her husband had done.

Her thoughts were once again interrupted by the man behind the bar. "That's the right amount," he said kindly, showing her the money he'd taken from her purse.

"I'll believe you – this time," she teased.

He pretended to be wounded. "I'm a honest man!" he protested merrily. She heard herself give a girlish giggle and once again she felt Jean's disapproving frown boring into her back.

She told herself she should be sensible – after all, he was a barman, he was paid to be friendly. Seeing his name badge, she couldn't resist asking: "How long have you been working here, Danny?"

He smiled pleasantly and she noticed that he had gorgeous dimples. His eyes twinkled roguishly: "Three seasons now. Seems like a life sentence."

Judith looked through the large window at the mighty Atlantic waves rolling into the bay, and said: "I can think of worse places to spend my time."

His expression changed and she guessed that underneath his blarney he respected his beautiful surroundings. He nodded: "It's impressive all right."

She found her gaze straying toward his left hand, but there was no wedding band there. "Are you from around here?" she asked.

He nodded: "Born and bred."

She loved his Irish brogue and the way his eyes held her gaze.

"Where are ye from?" he inquired, tilting his

PIC: KATE DAVIES

Judith's stomache did a somersault

head towards where Jean was sitting, waiting for her drink.

"London," she replied, feeling herself going pink at his interest.

"I have a sister living in London," he told her and they continued to chat with ease until he asked: "Is your husband with you?"

Judith felt a lump in her throat: "No. He passed away a few years ago."

Danny blushed furiously. "I'm so sorry," he stammered. "I saw your wedding ring and presumed..."

She regained her composure and felt glad that she had the ability to put the handsome man at ease. "Don't worry," she smiled reassuringly. He was

clearly still embarrassed so she continued: "Are you in a relationship?"

His confidence restored, he shook his head and laughed: "No. Who would have me?"

Judith's stomach did a somersault and she felt goose bumps on her arms. She looked quickly over her shoulder to see Jean striding toward them with a face like thunder. Why couldn't Jean accept that she was just having a bit of fun? Since Rex had died Judith missed being a woman who revelled in male attention. Her husband had always been an old-fashioned romantic, knowing when to shower her with compliments and kisses.

Maybe chatting up the barman had been a bit out of character, but she had just felt the need to enjoy some masculine flattery...

Jean grabbed the drinks and pulled her firmly away from the bar, saying: "For goodness' sake, Mother, remember you'll be seventy-five next birthday!"

Wednesday
1

Thursday
2

Friday
3

Saturday
4

Sunday
5

Monday
6
Summer Bank Holiday (Scotland)

Tuesday
7

Wednesday
8

Thursday
9

Friday
10

Saturday
11

Sunday
12
London Olympic Games' closing ceremony

Monday
13

Tuesday
14

Wednesday
15

Thursday
16

Friday
17

Saturday
18

Sunday
19

Monday
20

Tuesday
21

Wednesday
22

Thursday **23**	Tuesday **28**
Friday **24**	Wednesday **29**
Saturday **25**	Thursday **30**
Sunday **26**	Friday **31**
Monday **27** *Summer Bank Holiday*	

Poem of the month

PIC: ISTOCKPHOTO

The village fête

Home-made jams from the Women's Guild,
Pony rides in the adjoining field,
Small children who just can't wait
For candy floss at the summer fête.

Floral bouquets in the large marquee,
Tempting cakes in the tent marked 'Tea',
Enormous vegetables on display,
Grown with pride for this special day.

Three balls for 10p at the coconut shy,
Roll up, roll up. 'Let's have a try!
Or how about hoopla, throwing a ring?
Look at those prizes that we might win.'

The fête's nearly over, it's the end of the day.
Stalls to pack up and then put away.
Let's count the takings; they look good.
We all hoped and prayed that they would.

Now there's money to spend on our village hall,
With maybe some left to repair the church wall.
The villagers leave with a feeling of cheer,
Soon to start planning again for next year.
Pat Rolfe, Hornchurch, Essex

My Teenage Years
On our bikes

Being a member of Shepperton Youth Club was the best thing about my teenage years. Homework was rushed through as quickly as possible (or finished on the back seat of the school bus the next morning) so that I could get down there to meet my friends. Our innocent pleasures included table tennis, darts, snooker and drama.

We taught ourselves to jive and went in for all-night dance competitions, trying to impress the judges with daring moves, such as being swung up over your partner's head or down and through their legs. As all the competitions were knockout events we had to keep going without a refreshment break (just a can of coke on a table nearby).

We all had ponytails and flat shoes and when we

Mary (right) and friends at the Shepperton Youth Club annual dance in 1956

twirled we showed off our suspenders and stocking tops. (My father would have died if he had known!) Sometimes we wore skin-tight jeans which we shrank by sitting in a very hot bath with them on. I had to creep out in the evening without Dad getting a glimpse of them.

The Youth Club had a cycle section, too. When I was 15 and had to go into hospital in Harefield, my friend Janet got all the boys and girls to cycle there to visit me. The sister on the ward couldn't believe her eyes when around 25 teenagers appeared. She made them all sit outside on the grass and allowed me to go outside and join them.

Mary Archer, Shepperton, Middx

Bird of the week

PIC: ISTOCK

Dipper

One of the thrilling sights of a walk beside a fast-flowing river in the north and west of the country is this small, brown bird with its white throat and breast hopping from stone to stone and diving into the torrent. Dippers eat aquatic invertebrates, freshwater shrimps and small fish and search for them by walking under the water, grasping the stones. They even use their wings to hold their position in the stream and most of their food is swallowed under the water.
From Bird Watching magazine (www.birdwatching.co.uk)

Bright ideas

If you find that you constantly tear your washing up gloves due to having long nails turn them inside out and stick a plaster strip across the top of each finger. This will lengthen the life of your gloves saving you money in the long run.

I wish I'd said that

"Don't let your mind wander
– it's too little to be let out alone."

Only in Britain

Toe wrestling

Just when you think Britain can't get any more bonkers, you stumble across the World Toe Wrestling Championships. Apparently, founded in the Seventies, when George Burgess wanted to give England a chance at being world champions in at least one sport. Ironically a Canadian soon swiped the title!

Our Tune

Friendly Persuasion – Pat Boone

Back in the Fifties, a young man asked me to the cinema to see Friendly Persuasion. We loved the film, which was about a Quaker family who used 'thees' and 'thous'. Afterwards, when we felt romantic, one would say, "I love thee" and the other would answer, "Thee I love".

Doreen Duguid, Darlington

Photo I can't throw away

This photo was taken in 1936 when my brother and I were convalescing in a home in Bognor Regis following winter ailments. This was quite an adventure as it was the first time we had seen the sea, and we would walk, crocodile fashion, along the promenade with our carers. We had great fun, including dressing up as bluebells made from crêpe paper by the nursing staff, as shown in the photograph.

William Cooper, Ravensden, Bedfordshire

Recipe of the week

Tomato and Goats' Cheese Bruschetta

Serves: 4
Preparation time: 5 minutes
Cooking time: 10 minutes (plus 10 minutes cooling)

◆ 8 thick slices cut from a part-baked Ciabatta loaf
◆ 2 tbsp olive oil or pesto
◆ 150g soft goats' cheese
◆ 250g pack of cherry tomatoes
◆ Fresh basil leaves

1 Preheat oven to 190°C/375°F/Gas Mark 5. Arrange the slices of bread onto a baking sheet and drizzle with the oil or pesto. Bake for 5-10 minutes, or until golden brown and crisp. Remove from the heat and allow to cool slightly.
2 When ready, spread with the goats' cheese and top with halved cherry tomatoes and fresh basil. Sprinkle with salt and black pepper and serve immediately.

◆ **Top tip:** Replace the goats' cheese with mozzarella cheese if you're not a fan.
© Flour Advisory Bureau, www.fabflour.co.uk

My Teenage Years
Got ahead - got a hat

Having passed the 11-plus, my friend Rosalind and I attended a Technical High School in Leytonstone, three miles from our home in Leyton. Other pupils travelled much longer distances as the school had an excellent reputation. Many of them lived in Essex in houses whereas Rosalind and I were brought up in flats with no bathrooms (a bus to the local public baths was our regime, or a tin bath in front of the fire).

The better-off girls had uniforms in a slightly different shade of grey as their parents could afford to buy them from the official supplier – Harrods. Every year in June a sales team arrived from the famous

Brenda (left) proudly wearing her school hat

department store to take orders for new uniforms.

Not having that sort of money, parents from Leyton resorted to the local school outfitters. Mum made my dresses which were a perfect match and (oh joy!) my hat was from Harrods. It lasted six years until the day I left school when it was covered with everyone's signatures. I still have it.

However, from the moment we walked through the school gates, we were all equal. Those of us who came from poorer homes were never ridiculed, or made to feel inferior, despite the difference in our uniforms. We were strictly disciplined to learn, enjoy sport and work hard. I was a very shy girl but the experience helped to transform me into a confident young lady, able to take on whatever was out there, beyond the school gates.

Brenda Wilshere, Chingford

Bird of the week

PIC: ISTOCK

Yellowhammer

As the name implies, the males of this species appear as bright flashes of pale yellow singing from the top of a bush in arable countryside. They live in most of Britain and Ireland all year round, although they only spend the summer in the Pennines and Highlands of Scotland and they're not found at all on the Inner Hebrides or Orkney. The song of the Yellowhammer is often described as sounding as if the bird is calling 'a little bit of bread and no cheese'.
From Bird Watching magazine (www.birdwatching.co.uk)

Bright ideas

To stop raisins and other preserved fruits sinking to the bottom of cakes, dust them with flour before adding them to the mixture. It's not just raisins this rescues; it works just as well with chocolate chips and nuts too.

I wish I'd said that

"I'm a marvellous housekeeper. Every time I leave a man I keep his house." **Actress Zsa Zsa Gabor, well known for having married nine times.**

Only in Britain

Scary scarecrows

Head down to Kettlewell in the Yorkshire Dales during August and you'll be forgiven for thinking something strange is going on. A relatively new tradition, the annual Kettle Scarecrow Festival is delightful. Follow the Scarecrow Trail and you'll come across all kinds of characters – some easier to spot than others!

Our Tune

Summer Holiday – Cliff Richard

In 1963 my Dad invented the people carrier. He bought an old Atlas van, bolted some second-hand bus seats to the floor and off we went on holiday, singing 'Summer Holiday' all the way. There were nine of us in total, heading for an eight berth caravan!

Bren Morris, St Albans

Photo I can't throw away

I would like to share this photo with you. I am in the middle, my cousin, Jean, to my left and her brother, Barry, to the right. It was taken in 1947 at Skegness. We never had a lot of money when we were kids but we never ever missed a holiday to the seaside. Our parents worked hard all year so when it was pit week we all went to Skegness or Mablethorpe. We were as happy as Larry.

Josephine Clifton, Hucknall, Nottinghamshire

Recipe of the week

Apple and Pear Smoothie

Serves: 2
Preparation time: 5–10 minutes
(plus 1–2 hours chilling)

◆ 1 ripe banana, peeled and diced
◆ 2 Golden Delicious apples, peeled, cored, and coarsely diced
◆ 1 ripe pear, peeled, cored, and coarsely diced
◆ 250ml vanilla low-fat yogurt or soy yogurt
◆ 250ml apple juice
◆ Pinch ground cinnamon

1 Combine all the ingredients in a food processor or a blender and blitz until smoothly puréed. Alternatively, place in a container and process with a hand blender. Chill if you like it cold or serve immediately over ice in tall glasses.
© South Africa Apples and Pears

My Teenage Years
No 'hanky panky'

Ann and friend on a tor in Dartmoor, 1955

This photo was taken of me (on the right) with a friend on holiday in Devon in 1955, the same year that I started work, aged 16. As soon as I received my first wage packet, I bought a record player on HP (Hire Purchase) with my father as guarantor. The only record I could afford to buy was Red Sails in the Sunset which I played over and over again and must have driven my parents mad.

Money was very tight as we were expected to contribute to the household budget from our wages. I had to make my clothes and that included knitting jumpers and cardigans. Our dresses were pinched in at the waist and worn over voluminous petticoats which we rinsed in sugar water to stiffen them.

Curly hair was fashionable so we used home perms which made the house smell of ammonia all day. If you misjudged the timing of the perm, the result was a frizz and then there would be tears. We also wailed over our adolescent spots and blemishes.

With our girlfriends, we used to catch a bus to dances held at different town halls in the area. Hopefully, we'd meet a new boyfriend there who would escort us home on the bus. One of our parents would be waiting up to see us safely indoors and ensure that no 'hanky panky' occurred!

It seemed a very carefree time despite the restrictions.

Ann Davies, Milton Keynes

Bird of the week

PIC: ISTOCK

Rook

These big, noisy black birds have a lot of character and intelligence. In some recent scientific studies they have even proved that they can make simple tools of sticks and wire using their beaks, in order to make an item of food more accessible. Rooks always nest in a colony, at the tops of a group of tall trees, and in the autumn if there's a strong wind they flock together in huge aerial displays, almost as if they were playing in the gales.
From Bird Watching magazine (www.birdwatching.co.uk)

Bright ideas

Need your knives sharpened but don't have an expensive knife sharpener? Simply use the unglazed bottom of a ceramic or porcelain mug instead. Hold your knife at an angle to the base of the mug and start sharpening as you would normally.

I wish I'd said that

"I still have a full deck – I just shuffle slower now."
Unknown author.

Only in Britain

Gravy wrestling

As if toe wrestling wasn't strange enough, gravy wrestling – surely not? But yes, this is a crazy culinary competition where contestants wrestle in gravy for two minutes. This unlikely event forms part of the annual Pennine Lancashire Festival of Food & Culture. A waste of perfectly good gravy, but very entertaining.

Our Tune

Tie a Yellow Ribbon – Dawn featuring Tony Orlando

I first met my husband at a dance in 1973. He asked me to dance, and this tune was playing. There was an old flame at the same dance, and my mother told me to make my mind up, as she didn't want two young men calling at the door!

Ann Rowlatt, Deeping St James, Lincs

Photo I can't throw away

This photo of four friends, about 20/21 years old, was taken on a day trip to Weymouth in August 1951. Clothes rationing had finished in 1949 and although we didn't earn very much, mostly making do with basic pencil skirts with tops, blouses and cardigans, we loved fashion and did our best. I am second on the left and was wearing a green skirt, white top and a green patterned paisley scarf.

Colleen Walker, Salisbury, Wiltshire

Recipe of the week

Beetroot Salad with Sultanas and Basil with Lemon Croutons

Serves: 4
Preparation time: 10 minutes
Cooking time: 3–5 minutes

◆ 2 thick slices of 1-day old granary bread, crusts removed
◆ 125ml (5 fl oz) olive oil
◆ finely grated rind and juice of 1 lemon
◆ 2 tbsp balsamic vinegar
◆ 400g cooked beetroot (not in vinegar), cubed
◆ 75g feta cheese
◆ 50g sultanas
◆ Large handful fresh basil leaves

1 Cut the slices of bread into 1cm (1/2 inch) pieces. Then heat three tablespoons of the oil in a large non-stick frying pan. Add the bread pieces and sprinkle over the lemon rind. Cook over a medium heat for three minutes, or until they are crisp and have a nutty golden colour.
2 Tip the bread onto some kitchen paper and season to taste and set aside until needed.
3 To make the dressing, place the balsamic vinegar in a screw-top jar with the lemon juice and remaining olive oil. Season to taste, replace the lid and shake well to combine.
4 Just before serving, assemble the salad by placing the beetroot cubes on a large serving plate and crumble over the feta cheese. Then sprinkle the sultanas on top with the croutons and basil leaves. Drizzle over the dressing and serve. Ideally outside with a glass of white wine alongside it.

◆ **Top tip:** This salad makes a great packed lunch. Simply take the dressing along separately and drizzle it over just before serving.
© Ainsley Harriott for the Flour Advisory Bureau, www.fabflour.co.uk

My Teenage Years
Doing my bit

In 1942 I'd reached the magical age of 16. I was doing a job I loved but it was wartime and everyone had to be doing work of national importance. I was directed to a local factory where I became an electric welder. I quite liked the work which included doing the final weld on the inch-thick seams of tank turrets and armoured cars.

I applied to join the Women's Land Army and passed my medical with flying colours. After two successful interviews I was told to go home and wait for further instructions. While I was waiting, I went with my mother to work in the local hop fields. Some of the other workers were prisoners of war who lived in a very comfortable hut and had a cat that didn't understand a word of English.

I still hadn't heard from the Land Army when the Labour Exchange sent for me, wanting to know why

NAAFI Gang, Poperinge Barracks, Arborfield, Berks
– Mrs E A Collins (left)

I was not in the Forces or doing other work to help the war effort. I explained my situation and the young man behind the counter said he would check. He retired to a room at the rear of the office and returned with a form which he pushed in front of me, saying: "Sign here, please." We were naïve in those days and trusted our peers so I signed without reading it.

Two weeks later I found myself working in the NAAFI in Salisbury, on my way to another life and further adventures.

Mrs E A Collins, Grantham

Bird of the week

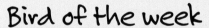

Green Woodpecker

PIC: ISTOCK

This is the biggest of the three types of woodpeckers that breed in Britain. With its green wings, yellowish-green rump and bright red head it is unmistakable prodding around on lawns and pastures or in woodland leaf litter, hunting for its favourite food – ants. If startled, they fly away with a bounding, undulating flight and their call is a laughing 'yaffle'. They are found in the lowlands all over most of Britain, but not in the far north of Scotland or in Northern Ireland.
From Bird Watching magazine (www.birdwatching.co.uk)

Bright ideas

If you need to give your grandchild some unpleasant tasting medicine, getting them to place an ice cube on their tongue beforehand will numb the tongue and lessen the taste of the potion. An ice cube also proves handy in numbing the skin around a splinter before you remove it.

I wish I'd said that

"I never forget a face, but in your case I think I'll make an exception." **Groucho Marx**

Only in Britain

St Bartholomew's Day fun

In Sandwich, Kent, St Bartholomew day (August 24) celebrations include children running around the church of St Barts and being rewarded with a current bun. Adults are given a biscuit stamped with the Sandwich coat of arms – thankfully they don't have to run anywhere for it!

Our Tune

This Is My Lovely Day – A P Herbert and Vivian Ellis

I was a teenager when I heard this and said I would have it played at my wedding. Little did I know I would have to wait until I was 76 for the wedding! I married Clive in 2010 in Gretna Green. And yes, this piece of music was played.

Rita Beesley, Crowborough, Sussex

Photo I can't throw away

This photo was taken during the Summer of 1930 on a family day out at Southend. This was an annual treat, paid for by my Grandfather. My Mother is on the left at the back holding me, and my older sister is in front of us holding the bucket and spade. My Grandmother is third from the left at the back. These were happy times, and that is why I can't throw this photo away.

Dorothy Edney, Canvey Island, Essex

Recipe of the week

Healthy Fruit Nut Muffins

Makes: 12 muffins
Preparation time: 15 minutes
Cooking time: 20-25 minutes
(plus 10 minutes cooling)

◆ 250g self-raising flour
◆ 75g dark muscovado sugar
◆ 1 tsp cinnamon
◆ 1 tsp baking powder
◆ 1/4 tsp salt
◆ 1 egg, lightly beaten
◆ 200g low-fat yogurt
◆ 125g butter, melted
◆ 2 tsp vanilla extract
◆ 50g carrot, grated
◆ 100g apple, peeled and grated
◆ 100g pecans, coarsely chopped
◆ 75g raisins
◆ 75g dried cranberries
◆ 50g desiccated coconut

1 Pre-heat the oven to 200°C/400°F/Gas Mark 6. Oil a 12-holed muffin tin with a little vegetable oil or line with paper muffin cases.
2 In a large mixing bowl, combine the flour, sugar, cinnamon and baking powder. Add a pinch of salt and then add the egg, yogurt, butter and vanilla extract and mix with a wooden spoon until just mixed.
3 Stir in the remaining ingredients until just combined. You should be left with a thick dough.
4 Fill each muffin hole with the mixture and bake for 20-25 minutes, or until the top is golden brown. Cool on a wire rack for 5-10 minutes and serve warm for the best taste.

◆ **Top tip:** These make a great breakfast on the go and will keep fresh stored in an airtight container for up to 3 days.
© Nielsen-Massey Vanillas, www.nielsenmassey.com

My Teenage Years
Cilla, my style icon

'**A**s I walk along, I wonder what went wrong
With our love, a love that was so strong'.
I have only to hear Del Shannon singing
Runaway to be instantly transported back to our local
coffee bar, Bill's in Brighouse, West Yorkshire, where
I used to listen to the jukebox while drinking hot lime
and blackcurrant. My favourite pop song was Billy
Fury's Last Night was Made for Love.

I wore dresses in the style made popular by Cilla
Black – Empire line trimmed with broderie anglais at
the cuffs and hem, worn with a belt around the hips. I
also liked low-waisted dresses with a sticky-out skirt
and a net petticoat. My favourite was plain pink with
a lime-green petticoat that scratched my legs, but I
happily put up with the discomfort. It was the fashion

Cilla Black inspired Patricia's youthful style

to wear matching clothes, so my boyfriend Bill (now
my husband) and I wore the same red and yellow
jumpers, knitted by me.

I always saved up to pay for my holidays. When I
was still at school I worked on Saturdays in the toy
department of the local Co-op. Later, I worked in a
bank and had two weeks holiday a year. The first week
was spent buying new clothes, Quickies eye make-up
remover pads and suntan cream in readiness for the
second week which was spent at Skegness.

Patricia Mason, Skipton, N Yorkshire

Bird of the week

PIC: ISTOCK

Kingfisher

Who can fail to be excited if they catch a glimpse
of brilliant blue and orange flashing along the
side of a slow-moving stream? Although the
Kingfisher comes from a large family of fish-
catching birds, there is only one type in the
UK. They nest in holes in a sandy riverbank,
excavating the soil with their beaks to make a
tunnel approximately two feet long. Choosing
a fish-rich territory for breeding is vital as each
chick eats up to 18 sticklebacks or minnows a day.
From Bird Watching magazine (www.birdwatching.co.uk)

Bright ideas

When oven-baking or grilling vegetables, don't save
the seasoning till after they cook. Beforehand, sprinkle
them with salt, ideally sea salt, as this helps draw out the
moisture so they caramelise to perfection.

I wish I'd said that

"Everyone probably does have a book in them, but in
most cases that's where it should stay."
**Author and journalist Christopher Hitchens'
response to the suggestion that anyone can
write a book.**

Only in Britain

Horn dance

First performed in 1226, this eccentric custom takes place every September in Abbots Bromley, Staffordshire. The Horn Dance is made up of six costume-wearing men carrying large antlers, a Maid Marian (a man dressed as a woman), a fool, a hobby horse and a youngster complete with bow and arrow.

Our Tune

I'd Be Far Better Off Without You – Sandy Shaw

I shall never forget our first Christmas of married life. I was a Sandy Shaw fan, and kept singing 'Girl Don't Come'. My husband bought it for me, but gave it to me B side up – 'I'd Be Far Better Off Without You'! It still gets mentioned after 48 years.

Janet Knapp, Bromley

Photo I can't throw away

At 16 a friend and I travelled from Bournemouth to Devon to stay with an Aunty of hers for a holiday. As you can see by the photo, we had such fun. I wonder whose hats they were?! I suppose I'll never know, but it's fun to look back on all the same. After this photo was taken, I joined the WRAF at 17 and had three years in Cornwall – I love that part of the world.

Margaret Knowles, Ferndown, Dorset

Recipe of the week

Sprouting Broccoli and Chickpea Frittata

Serves: 4
Preparation time: 10 minutes
Cooking time: 35 minutes

- 175g sprouting broccoli, each stem cut in half
- 2 tbsp olive oil
- $1/2$ medium red onion, finely chopped
- 1 medium red pepper, finely chopped
- 1 large clove garlic, finely chopped
- $1/2$ tsp smoked paprika
- 125g chickpeas, drained
- 2 tbsp fresh coriander, finely chopped
- 7 large eggs, lightly beaten and well seasoned

1 Preheat the oven to 190°C/375°F/Gas Mark 5 and lightly grease a ceramic baking dish, approximately 26 x 16 cm (10 x 6 inch), or an 18 cm (7 inch) loose-bottomed cake tin.
2 In a large saucepan of boiling water, parboil the broccoli for 2-3 minutes, drain and set aside.
3 Then heat $1^{1}/2$ tablespoons of the oil in a large frying pan and sauté the red onion and pepper for 5 minutes, or until soft. Add the garlic, paprika and chickpeas and cook for a further 2 minutes before adding the coriander.
4 Spread this mixture over the cooking vessel and place the broccoli on top and pour over the beaten eggs. Bake the frittata for 25 minutes, or until set and cooked through. Serve immediately with a fresh green, dressed salad.

© Tenderstem Broccoli, www.tenderstem.co.uk

Vintage teacup candles

These gorgeous teacup candles will look lovely in your home and make great gifts too

Takes 1 hour

◆ Scour charity shops and car boots for pretty china teacups and matching saucers.

You will need:

Vintage teacups
Wax pellets (1lb of wax will make 4 teacup candles)
Stearin
Medium lead-free wire wick
Pink candle dye
Bamboo skewer or straw, cut in half
2 old saucepans, one larger than the other
Old plastic jug

1 Cut a piece of wick about 5cm longer than the height of your teacup and tie it onto a skewer. Then balance the skewer on top of the cup with the longer end of the wick dangling inside.

2 Next, quarter fill the larger saucepan with cold water. Place the wax into the smaller pan and then place it inside the large pan, resting on a trivet if necessary. Gently bring the water to the boil and simmer on a low heat until the wax melts.

3 When the wax becomes molten add one tablespoon of stearin per pound of wax, which will improve the burning quality of your finished candle. Add your candle dye if you want your candle to be coloured.

4 Once the wax has completely melted, pour it into an old plastic jug and then pour straight way into your teacup. Leave to cool, but if a well forms around the wick, top up with a little more hot wax. Once your candle has cooled completely, untie the wick from the skewer and trim.

For more great craft projects and all your crafting supplies call 01202 596100 or visit www.hobbycraft.co.uk.

Quiz of the month

Can you guess the famous television presenters behind these well known British quiz and panel shows?

1 Who presented Take Your Pick between 1955 and 1968?

2 Name the late television presenter, son of Ted Ray and host of Call My Bluff?

3 Name the journalist and satirist who presented Through the Keyhole?

4 The last host of Blankety Blank was Lily Savage, but can you name the British comedian behind the drag queen alter ego?

5 Can you name the longest running presenter of Family Fortunes?

6 Name the English television personality who presented Play Your Cards Right?

7 Who was the original host of Ask the Family?

8 Name the 'Queen of Mean' Weakest Link presenter?

9 Can you name the very first and longest running presenter of Countdown?

10 Before they started using guest presenters, who was the original presenter of Have I Got News For You?

11 Who presented the radio and television series of Whose Line is it Anyway?

12 Name the Capital Radio DJ who hosts Who Wants To Be A Millionaire.

13 Name the original Mastermind presenter who was well known for saying, 'I've started so I'll finish'.

14 Do you know the first presenter of Blockbusters?

15 Who was the host of What's My Line after Gilbert Harding?

16 Bruce Forsyth was the original host of The Generation Game, but can you name any of the others?

17 This television presenter hosted Give Us A Clue between 1984 and 1992, but was better known for interviewing celebrities on his own chat show – can you name him?

18 Name the professional tennis player and host of A Question of Sport.

19 Can you name the presenter of Deal or No Deal?

20 Name the Blind Date television presenter who was well known for saying, 'What's your name and where d'ya come from?'

ANSWERS: 1) Michael Miles 2) Robin Ray 3) Sir David Frost 4) Paul O'Grady 5) Les Dennis 6) Bruce Forsyth 7) Robert Robinson 8) Anne Robinson 9) Richard Whiteley 10) Angus Deayton 11) Clive Anderson 12) Chris Tarrant 13) Magnus Magnusson14) Bob Holness 15) Eamonn Andrews 16) Roy Castle, Larry Grayson or Jim Davidson 17) Michael Parkinson 18) Sue Barker 19) Noel Edmonds 20) Cilla Black

Saturday **1**	Wednesday **12**
Sunday **2**	Thursday **13**
Monday **3**	Friday **14**
Tuesday **4**	Saturday **15**
Wednesday **5**	Sunday **16**
Thursday **6**	Monday **17**
Friday **7**	Tuesday **18**
Saturday **8**	Wednesday **19**
Sunday **9**	Thursday **20**
Monday **10**	Friday **21**
Tuesday **11**	Saturday **22**

Sunday **23**	Thursday **27**
Monday **24**	Friday **28**
Tuesday **25**	Saturday **29**
Wednesday **26**	Sunday **30**

PIC: ISTOCKPHOTO

Autumn takes
the stage

Shadows lengthen o'er the land
As Summer now takes Autumn's hand.
Together they walk on a while,
Before she leaves him with a smile.

Her scented beauty slowly fades
As time matures her pretty maids.
Then magic Autumn casts his spell
To gild each wooded slope and fell.

He paints the leaves with bronze and gold,
Bids fiery images unfold,
Unveils his glorious exhibition
And steals the show, this great magician.

Now, branches hung with garnets bright
Reveal old Autumn's wondrous might.
His endless bounties freely flow
To quell the wrath of Winter's snow.

Kay Spurr, Kirkby Stephen, Cumbria

My Teenage Years
Yankee-doodle-dandy!

In 1939 when the Second World War broke out, I was 15. I'd had to leave school the year before because my mother was ill and I needed to start work. My first job was in a rubber mill in Edinburgh but by the time I was 18 I was helping the war effort by working in a factory soldering condensers to put in radios for bombers.

I remember that the outside of the factory was camouflaged in dark greens and browns to make it look like a forest to German aircraft. Inside, in spite of the flames that heated the soldering irons, it was extremely cold. We girls hardly ever wore warm trousers as they were regarded as too 'common' for ladies. (Thank goodness that silly idea has long gone!)

As I loved dancing, Saturday nights in the village hall made up for the discomforts of the working week. In those days, the boys lined up on one side of the hall with the girls on the opposite side. When the accordion (or, if we were lucky, a band) started up, the boys would come over and politely invite a girl to dance. If she didn't want to, she would refuse equally politely.

A youthful Christina enjoyed all types of dancing

Then along came the Americans (or the Yanks, as they were known) and introduced us to the jitterbug. How well I remember being thrown to the left and right, up in the air, then through the legs of my partner!

Christina Gibbs, Lanark

Bird of the week

PIC: ISTOCK

Lapwing

Look across a ploughed field or on the muddy banks of an estuary or marshland and you're almost bound to see Lapwings with their little punky tuft on the top of their heads. In flight, the birds are easily separated from pigeons and other flocking birds of a similar size because their wings are blunt so they look like a flying rectangle. We have 150,000 pairs breeding here, but they are joined in autumn by European birds that swell the numbers to two million.
From Bird Watching magazine (www.birdwatching.co.uk)

Bright ideas

When making a cake, spend at least three to five minutes on the butter and sugar combining stage. It may seem excessive but a lengthy stint at the creaming stage will ensure you get enough air bubbles into the mixture for a light and well-risen cake.

I wish I'd said that

"I'm trying to imagine you with a personality."

Only in Britain
Face pulling antics

Egremont, a small Cumbrian town, comes alive every September when the Egremont Crab Fair is held. Dating back to 1267, it's one of the oldest fairs in the world and is also home to the famous World Gurning Championships. Contestants battle it out by pulling the ugliest face they can.

Our Tune
Here In My Heart – Al Martino

My all-time favourite tune is Al Martino singing 'Here In My Heart'. I thought he had the best voice ever. Our next door neighbour had a record player and used to play this rather loudly. But I didn't care, I loved it. We, at that time, couldn't afford such luxury.

Valerie Temple, Great Dunmow, Essex

Photo I can't throw away

This is a photograph of my mother, Ivy Lambert, taken on September 7, 1909 to celebrate her 2nd birthday. She is wearing her best white cotton dress and pantaloons, made by her mother. Gran often told us about the long walk she had carrying Ivy from the tram stop to the photographer in Acton High Street for this special portrait to be taken.

**Mrs S Bliss,
Basingstoke**

Recipe of the week

Speedy Sparkling Summer Surprise

Makes: 1 large jug
Preparation time: 5-10 minutes

◆ 100ml (4 fl oz) Tequila
◆ 2 limes
◆ 325ml (13 fl oz) Rubicon sparkling guava
◆ 325ml (13 fl oz) Rubicon sparkling lychee
◆ 4 slices of fresh grapefruit, to decorate

1 Squeeze the juice out of the limes and pour into a large cocktail jug.
2 Pour in all the other liquid ingredients and then top up with ice cubes and stir until icy cold.
3 Add the slices of grapefruit just before serving and pour into long glasses.

◆ **Top tip:** To make this a non–alcoholic cocktail replace the Tequila with the same amount of sparkling apple juice. The grandkids and teetotal friends will love it!
© Rubicon exotic juices, www.rubiconexotic.com

My Teenage Years
Eau de rose petals

My friend Kathleen's Dad used to grow roses and I hit on the bright idea of making our own perfume with the petals. We spent a morning collecting a carrier-bag full of the most fragrant petals. We then took them to my house when there was no one at home (it was going to be our secret).

First, we chopped them up and put them into jam jars. When we had about two inches of petals in each jar we topped them up with water then sealed the lids. We stored them in shoe boxes under my bed and made a pact that we wouldn't look at them for three weeks. At the end of three weeks we went upstairs full of excitement, dying to smell our 'new creation'. We were nearly sick when we opened the jars to find that all we'd produced was a putrid, gooey mess.

When I was 14 I longed for a pair of seamed nylon stockings but my mother would not allow me to have them. However, my young Aunt and Uncle bought me a pair. I thought I was great when I went out with them on but when I got back I had a great big hole in them. My Uncle asked how this had happened and I

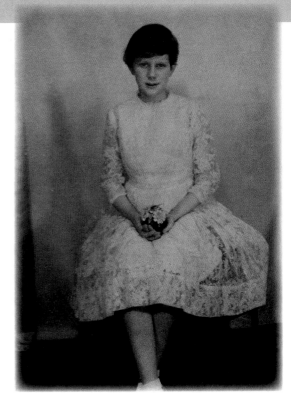

Climbing fences got Margaret into trouble

had to confess that I'd climbed over a fence to take a short cut home. I remember him telling me that young ladies do not climb fences – and it was quite a while before I got another pair.

Margaret Robertson, Chester-le-Street

Bird of the week

PIC: ISTOCK

Nuthatch

If you see a bird coming down a tree-trunk head first, it will almost certainly be a Nuthatch. These blue-grey birds with a pinky-brown breast and black eye stripe spend most of their time running up and down trees eating insects, nuts and seeds. They got their name from a corruption of 'nut hack' from their habit of wedging a nut in a crevice between branches and hacking at the shell with their powerful beak to break it open.
From Bird Watching magazine (www.birdwatching.co.uk)

Bright ideas

Left with a near-empty jar of hard and crystallised jam? Don't throw it out, just place the jar in a microwave, or oven for a while. The sugar will melt and the jam will be as good as new. Remember to leave to cool before polishing off the tasty preserve.

I wish I'd said that

"You see more of your children once they leave home." **Actress Lucille Ball reflects on reluctant birds leaving the nest.**

Only in Britain

Horseman's Sunday

It's not often you see a member of the church on horseback and if you're an equine devotee you'll love this. Taking place at Hyde Park Church, usually on the third Sunday in September, Horseman's Sunday celebrates horse riding in the heart of London with a gathering of more than 100 horses and riders.

Our Tune

Canadian Sunset – Andy Williams

In 1958 we went to New Zealand, and this tune was played on the voyage. The words are everything my husband and I meant to each other. Sadly he passed away in 2010, but I managed to get our song for him and it was played at his funeral.

Cecilia New, Maidenhead

Photo I can't throw away

Stan and I met when we were 16 and in spite of a lot of opposition from family, we stayed together and married in 1950. We have two sons, Colin and John, and two lovely grandchildren, Chris and Carrie. This photo was taken when Stan was doing his National Service – we were 18 at the time.

**Vi Hicks,
Dunstable, Beds**

Recipe of the week

Low-fat Cheese Loaf

Serves: 4-6
Preparation time: 10 minutes
Cooking time: 45 minutes

◆ 75g butter, softened
◆ 225g self-raising flour
◆ 1 tsp baking powder
◆ 1 tsp powdered mustard
◆ $1/2$ tsp salt
◆ Large pinch of black pepper
◆ 1 egg
◆ 75g low-fat mature Cheddar cheese, grated
◆ 8 tbsp milk

1 Preheat the oven to 180°C/350°F/Gas Mark 4 and grease and base-line a 450g (18 oz) loaf tin.
2 Place all the ingredients in a mixing bowl and beat together with a wooden spoon for 2-3 minutes, or until well mixed.
3 Spoon the mixture into the tin and bake for 40-45 minutes, or until cooked through and golden brown on top. Remove from the oven and leave in the tin for 5 minutes before turning out onto a wire rack to cool completely.
4 This tastes great sliced up and buttered alongside cold meats and a green salad as part of a picnic.
© Cathedral City, www.cathedralcity.co.uk

My Teenage Years
A likely lad

I was born in a pit village near Newcastle-on-Tyne in the Fifties and remember my older brothers in their Teddy Boy gear: drainpipe jeans, shoelace ties and crêpe-soled shoes known as 'brothel creepers'. They used milk to keep their flicked-back hairstyles in place – much to my Mother's anger when she found the milk bottle empty.

By the time I was 13 in 1964, The Beatles and Rolling Stones had exploded on to the music scene. When I was 15 I grew my hair halfway down my back which attracted much disapproving tutting. Then – shock, horror! – I dyed my auburn locks a brighter shade of red. My Father thought I was lost beyond saving, especially when I wanted to have a bath every day instead of once a week and started using deodorant and aftershave bought with money earned from my Saturday job.

My favourite clothes were platform shoes worn with flared trousers that reached to the floor so it

Teen style – but it was daily baths which caused a stir!

looked as though you had no feet. The must-have accessories were shirts patterned with little figures of elephants or birds. One fashion I never went for was the hippy 'flower people' look – embroidered jeans and a bell hung around your neck.

Our parents were in a state of shock but we were teenagers and we knew everything – they didn't have a clue. Fast forward two decades and the roles were reversed when I became the parent who 'didn't have a clue' and my teenage children rebelled in their own style.

Tim McMahon, Pennar, Pembrokeshire

Bird of the week

Ring-necked Parakeet
PIC: ISTOCK

These colourful parrots from the foothills of the Himalayas only started breeding in Britain at the end of the Sixties. Two stories are told about their origins: that a pair of birds escaped from Shepperton Studios during the filming of The African Queen; and that rock musician Jimi Hendrix released a pair from his London flat. Whatever the truth, they colonised successfully and can be found in large flocks in Greater London and south-east England, with birds now reported in almost every English county.
From Bird Watching magazine (www.birdwatching.co.uk)

Bright ideas

If you've forgotten to bring butter to room temperature for a recipe or for bread, take a glass bowl large enough to fit over the butter, fill with very hot tap water and leave for 5 seconds. Empty and place over the butter for softened butter in minutes.

I wish I'd said that

"Sit down and give your mind a rest."

Only in Britain

Kiss me quick

A stolen kiss from a chimney sweep on the way to her wedding used to mean good luck for brides. Nowadays it's not so common to see sweeps passing by, but brides can still hire a lucky sweep for their big day and who knows what luck it will bring?

Our Tune

People Will Say We're In Love from Oklahoma!

Starting work in a grown-up world in 1947 was so exciting. The musical 'Oklahoma' was wowing the audiences in London and this was my favourite song. I sang it all day at work and, no doubt, drove my workmates mad. I still get a thrill every time I hear it.

Mrs T McGowan, Bury

Photo I can't throw away

This was taken in September 1947. I was 18 years old and went to Butlin's at Skegness with two friends for my first holiday. We met these three lads on the first day and spent the whole week with them. When we left, one of them gave me a letter to read on the tram, saying he would always remember me as his Butlin's girlfriend. Of course, that was the last contact we had, but I never forget my Butlin's boyfriend.

Maureen Shallcross, Wakefield

Recipe of the week

Saintly Little Chocolate Cream Pots

Serves 6
Preparation time: 5 minutes
Cooking time: 15 minutes (plus 2 hours chilling time)

- ◆ 25ml (1 fl oz) skimmed milk
- ◆ 25ml (1 fl oz) low–fat whipping cream (at least 5% fat)
- ◆ 4 egg yolks
- ◆ 1 level tbsp granulated sweetener
- ◆ 150g dark chocolate

1 In a medium non–stick saucepan, gently bring the milk and cream to the boil. Then gradually whisk in the egg yolks one at a time, removing from the heat if it looks like it is going to curdle.
2 Place on another hob ring on a low heat stirring constantly for 5 minutes, or until the mixture coats the back of a spoon.
3 Break the chocolate into small pieces and add to the pan. Continue to stir until this is all melted, around 5 minutes.
4 Take the pan off the heat and add the sweetener. Whisk until the cream becomes light and fluffy and has cooled down slightly.
5 Pour the mixture into small serving glasses or ramekins and chill in the fridge for at least 2 hours before serving.

◆ **Top tip:** You can replace the sweetener with the same amount of caster sugar.
© Splenda. www.splenda.co.uk

My Teenage Years
'Sweet Little Sixteen'

Schoolgirl crushes changed frequently

The photo shows me (in the middle) with my friends, Pam and Chris. It was taken in the grounds of the all-girls grammar school where we were pupils. At the time, it was in the process of being turned into a comprehensive. Young workmen swarmed everywhere and suddenly school became more interesting!

We girls had crushes on boys but these changed frequently and were very innocent. I was euphoric whenever the current dreamboat noticed me and I felt despair when spots erupted on my face – then I felt I was the ugliest girl in the school.

Free from the constraints of school uniform, we wore jeans, baggy sweaters and duffle coats. But on Saturday nights we would get all dressed up in full skirts and petticoats to go dancing. My favourite place to dance was the local Palais and my favourite song was Sweet Little Sixteen. When the music started to play and the revolving lights sent a myriad rainbow colours round the walls I felt I had entered another world. Hollywood must surely be like this!

American influences were everywhere, from coffee bars to rock 'n' roll. James Dean and Elvis were our idols (although we loved Cliff as well). After school, some of us would sometimes meet up to go to a jazz club or to the local youth club. Now that we are all 70, we are still good friends. As we might have said back in 1956 – rock on!

Doreen Russell, Norwich

Bird of the week

PIC: ISTOCK

Blackcap
This little warbler has been nicknamed the Northern Nightingale because of the Blackcap's melodious piping song. Autumn and winter are a good time to see the birds with their pinky-grey breasts and dark wings. Males have a glossy black top to their heads, above the eyes, and females a red-brown one. Although many migrate away from the UK at the end of summer, an increasing number have been staying on and coming into gardens for the fruit and seed we put out as winter provisions.
From Bird Watching magazine (www.birdwatching.co.uk)

Bright ideas
If you don't have a lot of drying space, strip the material from an old umbrella and hang from a high rail, or washing line. This provides an excellent way to dry your smalls and free up room on the line for larger items.

I wish I'd said that
"They say old age is all in the mind, but the trick is to keep it from creeping down to your body."
Unknown author.

Only in Britain

Afternoon tea

Afternoon tea became fashionable in England during the 1880s, when society women would change into formal wear to enjoy their afternoon tea in the drawing room. Including sandwiches, scones, cakes and, of course, tea. It remains a terribly civilised affair today.

Our Tune

When Your Old Wedding Ring Was New – Jimmy Dean

We always went on coach holidays with friends. In the evenings we had sing-songs, and this was my Fred's song. Last year was Fred's 100th birthday, and sure enough he was asked to sing it. Tears rolled down our faces – he forgot some of the words but he made it.

Rene Holgate, Harlow

Photo I can't throw away

This is me in the Fifties in my husband's old Hillman Minx. We were courting then, and travelled many miles in it on trips to visit the coast, having lovely picnics along the way. My husband made a picnic table and we took a stove with us, cooking our food by the side of the road. The car didn't have a heater though, and I remember my legs always being cold! What memories this picture holds.

Jean Pearce, Dereham, Norfolk

Recipe of the week

Peppered Chicken and Pear Salad

Serves 4
Preparation time: 15 minutes
(plus 30 minutes marinating time)
Cooking time: 10 minutes

For the base:
◆ 2 large boneless, skinless chicken breasts cut into thick finger strips
◆ Juice of 1/2 lemon
◆ 1 tbsp olive oil
◆ 2 garlic cloves, crushed
◆ 1 tsp of cracked black pepper

For the dressing:
◆ 150g Lactofree Soft White Cheese
◆ 5 tbsp white wine
◆ 1 tbsp wholegrain mustard
◆ 1 small bunch fresh chives, finely chopped

For the topping:
◆ 2 baby gem lettuces, washed
◆ 2 ripe dessert pears, halved, cored and sliced
◆ 4 spring onions, chopped
◆ 4 rashers lean bacon, grilled until crispy

1 Put the chicken strips into a bowl and add all the other base ingredients. If time allows, chill and marinate for half an hour.
2 Then heat a large wok or non-stick frying pan. Add the chicken along with any leftover marinade and stir-fry for 5-7 minutes, or until the chicken is cooked through and set aside.
3 Meanwhile make the dressing, place the Lactofree cream cheese, white wine, mustard and 15ml/1tbsp cold water into a small pan and stir over a medium heat. Stir in the chives.

To serve: arrange the baby gem leaves, pear slices and spring onions into the middle of four serving plates. Top with the hot chicken and drizzle over the warm cheese dressing. Crumble over the crispy bacon and serve straight away.
© Lactofree Dairy products, www.lactofree.co.uk

Cuddly koala

◆ Try not to get your sugarpaste too wet, or the pieces will slide off rather than stick.

Cute and quirky, this sugarpaste creation would make a great cake topper

You will need:

65g lilac sugarpaste
Small amounts of white and black sugarpaste
Candy stick (from sweetshops nationwide)
Drinking straw (with the end cut at an angle)
Sharp pointed scissors
Thin palette knife (available from sugarcraft and art shops)
Heart cutter, 2.5cm (1inch)

Takes 30 minutes

1 Divide the lilac sugarpaste, taking about 25g for the body, then form this into an egg shape and push the candy stick into the top of the egg shape down through the middle of the body – this will give support.
Stick on a white heart shape for the tummy.

2 Divide the rest of the lilac paste into four balls. Take two of the balls and form each one into a carrot shape to make the legs. Mark two lines with a knife to make toes. Attach the legs by dampening the ends with a small paintbrush dipped in water.

3 Divide one of the remaining balls into two and make smaller carrot shapes for the arms. Again, mark the paws with a knife and join to the body. With the last ball make a circle and squash slightly so it's a rounded rectangle shape. Mark a smiley mouth with the cut end of the drinking straw and then attach the head to the body pushing onto the end of the candy stick.

4 Make two small white ovals for the ears. Stick on the sides of the head, pushing in gently to cup them, then snip around the edges with scissors to make it look like fur.

5 Finish by making a nose from a black oval shape and the eyes from two tiny balls of black paste. Make a baby koala in the same way, but use lighter coloured sugarpaste.

Sugar Animals (£4.99) by Frances McNaughton and published by Search Press is part of the Twenty to make easy craft series, call 01892 510850 or visit www.searchpress.com

Quiz of the month

Can you answer the questions about these children's television dramas? The answers are below if you get stuck.

PIC: REX/FEATURES

1 In Grange Hill, which well-known actor played Peter 'Tucker' Jenkins?

2 In The Famous Five, who owned a dog called Timmy?

3 Who is the head of the Secret Seven?

4 Who was the head teacher of Grange Hill in 1978?

5 In the Press Gang, what was the children's newspaper called?

6 Zammo Macguire was best known for his hard-hitting drug storyline in Grange Hill. But do you know the character's actual first name?

7 Name the author behind The Secret Seven and The Famous Five books?

8 For how many years had it been since anyone had stepped into the garden in The Secret Garden?

9 In the Famous Five, who's the oldest of the four children?

10 In Stranger on the Shore, where was Marie-Hèléne Ronsin from?

11 Where are the Secret Seven meetings held?

12 What was the name of the girl who went to live with her uncle in The Secret Garden?

13 Which Eastenders actress previously played Julie Craig in the Press Gang?

14 In Stranger on the Shore, Marie-Hèléne Ronsin went to live with a family in which British city?

15 In the Famous Five, what was the name of George's island?

16 Which Absolutely Fabulous actress played Lynda Day in Press Gang?

17 How many members of the Secret Seven can you name?

ANSWERS: 1) Todd Carty 2) George 3) Peter 4) Mr Starling 5) The Junior Gazette 6) Samuel 7) Enid Blyton 8) 10 years 9) Julian 10) France 11) Peter's shed 12) Mary Lennox 13) Lucy Benjamin 14) Brighton 15) Kirrin Island 16) Julia Sawalha 17) Peter, Janet, Pam, Barbara, Colin, Jack and George

Mrs Morgan's Secret

BY: JEAN HILL

Nobody knows why Edna's neighbour keeps herself to herself...

Johnny dawdled along carrying the loaf he'd fetched from the corner shop, picking the burnt bits from the top and eating them.

"Well, it's taken you long enough – and just look at this loaf! How many times have I told you not to do that?"

"Sorry, Mum," Johnny mumbled. "Mum! Mrs Morgan's front door is open and Barney is running round outside."

"Perhaps, she just nipped to the shop."

"No, I'd have seen her. Mrs Morgan's door is always shut…"

He was right thought Edna. Mrs Morgan, a widow, kept herself to herself. A brief 'good morning' was all the socialising she did. Glancing out, she saw Barney, a small, rough-haired terrier, chasing toffee papers in the gutter. Turning to her son, she said: "Johnny, see if you can catch Barney – the fish-man's van is due soon and he might get run over."

Mrs Morgan lived two doors away and sure enough the front door was wide open. Edna knocked tentatively. "Mrs Morgan, hello, it's Edna Jones. Are you all right?" There was no reply. Edna knocked again and stepped into the hallway of the small terraced house. It was spotlessly clean and tidy. She thought of her own home where Johnny's bicycle was propped up inside the front door and she was constantly wiping grubby fingerprints from the walls.

Edna ventured into the living room, equally neat except for a cardboard box in the middle of the floor. On it was written 'Ferguson 10-inch screen'. 'A television!' thought Edna, 'The only one in the street. Mr Morgan must have left her well off'.

She looked into the empty kitchen, then called up the stairs: "Mrs Morgan, it's Edna from down the road. Are you all right?" Thinking she heard a noise, she climbed the stairs, repeating: "It's all right, it's only me, Edna."

'Mr Morgan must have left her well off'

She pushed open the door to the front bedroom. No one there, nor in the bathroom. That left the back bedroom. 'She must be in here', thought Edna, bracing herself for what she might find. But even in her wildest dreams she wouldn't have anticipated the scene that met her eyes.

A young man was lying on a hospital bed with high metal sides. By the bed there was a bucket containing soiled pyjamas and a bowl of water in which a bar of soap was dissolving. His eyes opened wide with fear when he saw Edna, but she reassured him: "Don't be frightened. My name's Edna."

"Edna," he repeated.

"Yes, that's right. What's your name?"

"Edna," he replied.

"No, I'm Edna," she said pointing to her chest. "Who are you?"

"Mum!" screamed the lad. "Mum!"

"I'm here," came a quiet voice from the doorway. It was Mrs Morgan.

Later that day, when the pyjamas were blowing on the line and Barney was curled up in his basket, Edna and Mrs Morgan sat drinking tea. "When we moved here," Mrs Morgan began, "we'd been married for many years and thought we couldn't have children. But we had not been here long when I found I was expecting."

"New house, new baby," smiled Edna.

"Everything went well with the birth and the baby ate well and slept well; we couldn't believe how lucky we were. But there was something I couldn't put my finger on that didn't seem quite right. Mother's instinct, I suppose. Jim, my husband, thought I was worrying over nothing, but when little Harry didn't try to crawl, even he had to admit there was something wrong. I wanted to see a doctor but Jim said they would take him away from us."

"So you just carried on by yourselves?" asked Edna.

"Yes, and I managed quite well until Jim died, but lately I don't seem to have as much energy or patience as I used to and this morning, I'm ashamed to say, something snapped. Harry just wouldn't keep still while I tried to bathe him and for the first time, I

PIC: KATE DAVIES

slapped him."

Edna thought of all the times she had given Johnny a quick clip round the ear for some minor wrong-doing and put her hand over Mrs Morgan's.

"I shall never forget the look on his face. I ran out of the door and just kept going until I reached Jim's grave. I told Jim that I could not go on any more and it was all his fault for leaving me…"

Edna patted her neighbour's hand: "You're only human, you know, and it has all become too much for you. Now you need help. People round here aren't bad when you get to know them, any one of them would lend a hand. But first I think we should call the doctor."

Mrs Morgan was too exhausted to argue. The doctor arranged for Harry to go into a nursing home for a short while and assured her that when he came home someone would come every day to help with his care. Edna's husband volunteered to re-decorate the lad's room and Edna took Mrs Morgan on a shopping trip to buy new bedding and curtains. They had tea in Lyons Corner House, and Mrs Morgan felt she had rejoined the human race.

The television came into its own when all her neighbours and new-found friends crammed into Mrs Morgan's living room to watch the coronation of Queen Elizabeth. When they all left, Mrs Morgan thought how much her life had changed in a few short weeks, and Barney licked a salty tear from her cheek.

Monday

1

Tuesday

2

Wednesday

3

Thursday

4

Friday

5

Saturday

6

Sunday

7

Monday

8

Tuesday

9

Wednesday

10

Thursday

11

Friday

12

Saturday

13

Sunday

14

Monday

15

Tuesday

16

Wednesday

17

Thursday

18

Friday

19

Saturday

20

Sunday

21

Monday

22

Tuesday

23

Wednesday

24

Thursday

25

Friday

26

Saturday

27

Sunday

28

British Summer Time ends (clocks go back)

Monday

29

Tuesday

30

Wednesday

31

Hallowe'en

Poem of the month

A Hallowe'en tale

On the last of October
As day fades to night,
Clouds roll from the moon
That shows golden and bright.
And there, from the darkness,
Across the moon's face
Sails a black silhouette
From a faraway place.
There's a sharply hooked chin
And a tall pointed hat.
And riding behind her,
A furry black cat!
I am watching a witch
Riding high on her broom,
And swiftly behind her
(As though in a race)
Pass more silhouettes
Across the moon's face.
I don't care what you say
For I know what I've seen,
I'll be safely in bed
On the next Hallowe'en!
**Patricia Mason,
Skipton, N Yorkshire**

PIC: ISTOCKPHOTO

My Teenage Years
Hooray for pay day!

This picture was taken on my thirteenth birthday party at my gran's flat. We thought we looked pretty good in our stockings and short skirts.

From the age of 13 to 18, I was in foster care which had a big impact on my life. One of my foster homes was with a couple called Daphne and Colin. I loved being part of their family and helping Daphne in the kitchen. She showed me how to make milk jelly with evaporated milk which was easy and delicious. We are still in touch today and still swap recipes.

My friend Julie and I worked at a firm called Wingard in Chichester. On Fridays we had a half-day. After getting our pay packet at lunchtime we set off down the pub where we drank rum-and-cokes

Teenage party-goers felt they were very grown-up

before catching the train home to Southsea. On some weekends, we went dancing. A favourite place was the Bali Hai in Bognor. We wore halter-neck tops and very high wedge shoes. Anything we wore that was white glowed in the ultraviolet lighting.

We also used to go dancing at the Mecca ballroom in Portsmouth. I remember the ladies' toilets were very posh, with mirrors everywhere. We girls used to spend ages in there fixing our make-up, clothes and hair before going out to the dance hall where we all stood around in a large circle with our handbags in the middle. We had a lot of fun in those days.

Lynda Crossland, Portsmouth

Bird of the week

PIC: ISTOCK

Red Kite

Hunted to extinction in the UK by the end of the 19th century, the Red Kite is a magnificent chestnut red and white bird of prey. They have been gradually coming back thanks to a reintroduction programme started in the Eighties, with birds from Europe. Red Kites are mainly carrion eaters and were well known in medieval cities as sanitation operators, scavenging on the rubbish in the streets. Still under threat from egg collectors and illegal poisoned bait, the birds are nonetheless gradually becoming part of our wildlife hierarchy again.
From Bird Watching magazine (www.birdwatching.co.uk)

Bright ideas

Don't be blinded after chopping up chillies by mistakenly rubbing your eyes. Put a little bit of vegetable oil or olive oil on your fingers and rub for a minute before rinsing off using washing up liquid. The oil removes the tear inducing culprit – capsaicin.

I wish I'd said that

"The only time a women succeeds in changing a man is when he's a baby."
West Side Story star Natalie Wood.

Only in Britain

Conker madness

Where else but in Britain, would banging together seeds from horse chestnut trees be so entertaining? At this time of year, when conkers are everywhere, the game is still popular. With roots dating back to the 1800s, the World Conker Championships is held annually in autumn, at Ashton near Oundle, Northamptonshire.

Our Tune

I Wouldn't Trade You For The World – The Bachelors

Back in 1963, my husband was doing an unaccompanied tour to Aden with the RAF, and I had this played for him on BFBS radio. Needless to say it was always our tune from then on. Unfortunately, my husband passed away in April 2009 after almost 49 years of marriage.

Jean Pearson, Milton Keynes

Photo I can't throw away

Here is a photo of my paternal Grandmother and Grandfather, Amelia and Charles, with her brother Thomas in the early 1900s. I love how smartly dressed they all look, and what about the cigarettes? Not so politically correct these days! My Nan looks very confident with her two favourite men to protect her. She was 94 when she died – I was only 21 then, but I still miss her.

Catherine Hiscox, Hemel Hempstead

Recipe of the week

Cardamom Apples with Tuscan Oats

Serves: 4
Preparation time: 10 minutes
Cooking time: 20–25 minutes

- 4 dessert apples
- 1 tsp ground cardamom

For the oats:
- 75g porridge oats
- 50g butter
- 50g light brown sugar
- 50ml Oatly organic dairy-free alternative to cream (plus extra for serving)

1 Preheat the oven to 200°C/400°F/Gas Mark 6.
2 Cut the apples into segments discarding the core and place in a medium oven-proof dish. Stir in the cardamom.
3 Mix together all the ingredients for the Tuscan oats in a small saucepan and heat gently for 1 minute.
4 Spoon this over the apples and bake in the middle of oven for 15–20 minutes, or until the apples are tender and the top is golden brown.

- **Top tip:** You can use normal cream if you prefer.
© Oatly, www.oatly.co.uk

My Teenage Years
'Johnnie Remember Me'

I met my boyfriend John at a rock 'n' roll club in Bournemouth when he was doing National Service at a nearby army camp. He had a big motorbike and came from New Malden. When I went there on his bike, I used to wear my Dad's trousers and two pairs of long socks, thick tights and two or three jumpers. I looked like the Michelin Man.

An only child, he lived in a council house with his mother who weighed around 18 stone and was very possessive of her son. She would never go to bed while John and I were up, just in case we kissed or did something 'not right'.

Life for John was buying clothes, going dancing at the local Palais, working on motorbikes and meeting his mates in the pub. I just had to tag along and be quiet! However, he had a great sense of fun so life was never dull. For his 21st birthday in May 1958, Johnny wanted a double-breasted blazer

Eunice and Johnny in 1956

that cost around £12. As I was earning only £5 10s a week it was a big expense for me and I saved up for months to buy it.

Ironically, in August of that year he sent me a 'Dear John' letter in which he wrote that he was very fond of me and I was a lovely girlfriend but we lived too far apart and he had met a girl called Rita whose parents were very well off. So that was that!

Eunice Cranfield, Alicante, Spain

Bird of the week

PIC: ISTOCK

Starling

Regularly seen working as a team, Starlings march in lines up a lawn, or chattering noisily from trees. Autumn, however, brings the most spectacular sights as they gather in huge flocks at dusk to settle in a roost for the night. They come together gradually, forming great swirling clouds within which the birds move with co-ordinated grace, wheeling and swooping before coming in to huddle in woods or along the struts of a pier. This wildlife spectacle is known as a murmuration.
From Bird Watching magazine (www.birdwatching.co.uk)

Bright ideas

Many stocks, soups and mulled wines call for a herb or spice sachet, which is traditionally made from cheesecloth. If you don't have any lying around, a paper coffee filter, filled with the herbs and fastened at the top with twine works just as well.

I wish I'd said that

"I'm not as dumb as you look."
Bordering on rude, but effective!

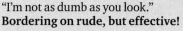

Only in Britain

Our daily bread

England is full of bread superstitions, including marking loaves with the sign of the cross before baking to prevent the devil sitting on and spoiling the loaf. Or, if you cut into a loaf and found a hole, a death would occur – a little vague if you think about it.

Our Tune

I Just Called To Say I Love You – Stevie Wonder

My husband was a long distance lorry driver and would work nights, staying away a lot. He used to call me every evening and sing this down the phone to me. We were married for 37 years, and now he has passed away it holds very dear memories for me.

Linda Taylor, Scunthorpe

Photo I can't throw away

This photo was taken in 1960, of my two sons, David and Alan, at a fancy dress party in the new community hall. David was five years old and was dressed as the Tonibell Cow. I made his outfit with the help of the regular driver who gave me some of the badges and cows. Alan was three years old and went as King Farouk.

Mrs O M Faint, Basildon

Recipe of the week

Beef Stew with Cheesy Dumplings

Serves: 4
Preparation time: 10 minutes
Cooking time: 2 hours (plus 45 minutes)

- ◆ 1 tbsp oil
- ◆ 500g diced casserole beef, rinsed and dried
- ◆ 2 large leeks, finely sliced
- ◆ 300g Chantenay carrots, peeled and halved
- ◆ 2 tbsp plain flour
- ◆ 500g ready–made pouch beef stock
- ◆ Splash of red wine, optional

For the dumplings:
- ◆ 175g self–raising flour, sieved
- ◆ 75g shredded suet
- ◆ 1 tbsp parsley, finely chopped
- ◆ 75g mature Cheddar cheese, grated
- ◆ Salt and pepper

1 Preheat the oven to 160°C/325°F/Gas Mark 3. Heat the oil on the hob in an oven–proof casserole dish and cook the beef in batches, until evenly browned. Remove from the pan and set aside.
2 Add the leeks to the pan and cook for 5 minutes, or until softened. Sprinkle over the flour and stir till the juices thicken. Stir in the stock and the red wine, if using. Add the cooked beef and carrots. Cover and bake for 2 hours 10 minutes.
3 Meanwhile, make the dumplings by mixing together all the ingredients in a bowl. Add enough water (about 3 tablespoons) to make soft, but not sticky dough. Lightly flour your hands and roll the dough into eight small balls.
4 When the stew is cooked, add these to the dish and cook for a further 15-20 minutes. Serve with greens and some crusty bread.

© Cathedral City, www.cathedralcity.co.uk

My Teenage Years
Riding pillion

In 1955 when I was 15 I had to be home by 9.30pm on the dot so I was always the first to leave my group of friends as I didn't want to risk being grounded by my Pop.

One evening after church club when a crowd of us were sitting around, putting the world to rights (complaining that our parents didn't understand us etc) one of the boys said: "Kay, it's half past nine, I'd better give you a lift home on my motor bike."

I jumped up with my heart in my mouth (because I was late – and also the boy was a bit special), gathered up my full skirt, and off we went. Arriving at my house, I let go of my skirt so I could jump off as soon as we stopped. This resulted in a nasty accident as the material wrapped itself round the rear wheel of the bike and left me with my petticoat flapping in the breeze.

I ran into the house, not sure whether I was more worried about being late or because my knickers

Trousers were a better mode of dress on a motorbike

were on show! I had to own up to my parents and my lovely Pop went to help the lad remove my skirt from his bike so he could go home.

After that, I was banned from riding motor bikes but I never lost my love of them and when I was 71 I had a fantastic ride on a 1974 Harley Davidson in Arizona (but that's another story).

Kay Beever, Rustington, W Sussex

Bird of the week

PIC: ISTOCK

Brambling

Shy little finches that breed in Scandinavia and Siberia, Bramblings come to spend the winter in our beech woodlands where they feed on the seeds. Their migrating flocks can number tens of thousands, even millions of birds. They can be seen in gardens when a harsh, cold snap forces them to search out a supplement to their food supplies. They often congregate with Chaffinches where they stand out as the more colourful birds because of the male's bright orange breast and white rump.
From Bird Watching magazine (www.birdwatching.co.uk)

Bright ideas

Don't spend money on expensive 'laundry water' to use while ironing. To make your clothes and sheets smell heavenly add a few drops of your favourite scent to the water in your iron.

I wish I'd said that

Man: Didn't we go out on a date once? Or was it twice?
Women: It must have been once. I never make the same mistake twice.

Only in Britain

October Plenty at Shakespeare's Globe

This autumn harvest celebration includes a Corn Queene effigy covered in produce from the local fruit and veg hub of Borough Market and a Berry Man who wears all kinds of foliage. Steeped in tradition it's a lovely day out with a procession, drama performances and even storytelling for the children.

Our Tune

Fools Rush In (Where Angels Fear To Tread) – Etta James

When my husband and I married in 1962, we were given our very first transistor radio, and took it with us on honeymoon. On arrival at our hotel I put the radio on, and this was the tune being played! We just looked at each other and burst out laughing.

Martie Hall, County Down

Photo I can't throw away

I left school in July 1939 intending to become a nurse, but found there was no training available for two years, so the best thing to do was to join the army, where I became a Kine Theodolite operator. As much of our work was outdoors, we were thankful to be given the men's battledress shown in the photograph. Later a thinner women's battledress was issued, but we hung on to our warm male uniform for as long as possible!

Chris Coxon, Weymouth

Recipe of the week

Galaxy and Vanilla Marble Cake

Makes: 1 loaf
Preparation time: 10 minutes
Cooking time: 1 hour 30 minutes

◆ 225g unsalted butter, room temperature
◆ 225g caster sugar
◆ 1 tbsp vanilla extract
◆ 75g Galaxy chocolate
◆ 1 tsp cocoa powder
◆ 4 eggs, beaten
◆ 225g self-raising flour

1 Preheat the oven to 180°C/350°F/Gas Mark 4 and lightly grease and base-line a 900g (2 lb) loaf tin.
2 Melt the chocolate in a small bowl over simmering water, but don't let the water touch the bowl. Leave to cool slightly.
3 Meanwhile, place the butter, vanilla extract and sugar in a large bowl. Cream together until the mixture is light and fluffy. Gradually add the beaten eggs, a little at a time, adding a little of the flour if the mixture starts to curdle.
4 Finally, fold in the flour and then spoon half the mixture into another bowl. Fold the melted chocolate and cocoa powder into one bowl of mixture.
5 Spoon alternate spoonfuls from each bowl into the loaf tin. When all the mixture has been used, drag a table knife through the mixture to help give a marbled effect.
6 Bake for 1¼ hours, or until a knife inserted into the cake comes out clean. Remove from the tin and leave to cool on a cooling rack.
© Galaxy, www.galaxychocolate.co.uk

My Teenage Years
Emergency exit

Compared with today's teenagers, I was very naïve. I didn't date anyone until after I left school although I did have a crush on a boy who went to the grammar school. He played the oboe in the school orchestra and I used to wait for him (accidentally on purpose) on Monday evenings when he came back from practice. It was all very innocent but when my Dad found out he banned me from seeing him again.

My next love was a boy I met at the youth club. I was still only 17 and not ready to commit, so he ended our romance. Feeling jilted, I moped around the house for weeks but eventually recovered, of course.

My friend and I used to go our local Palais de Danse in Ilford. One night we met a couple of lads and had a few dances with them but we decided we weren't keen. When they asked to see us home, we politely declined, but they were insistent. We didn't like being pressured so we hatched a plan.

Telling the lads that we'd get our coats then meet them outside, we slipped out of the emergency exit

Pat and her friend had to avoid the Palais for a while

at the back of the building and dashed round the corner to the bus stop, praying they wouldn't see us. From the top of the bus we could see them waiting and wondered how long they stood there. After that, we avoided the Palais for some weeks in case we bumped into them again.

Pat Rolfe, Hornchurch, Essex

Bird of the week

PIC: ISTOCK

Coal Tit

The least colourful of the tit family, the Coal Tit is nevertheless a very pretty little bird with its blue-black head and neck. Flocks of Coal Tits like to forage for food in deciduous woodland, keeping in touch with each other with constant seep-seep calls. We can attract them to our gardens by offering sunflower seeds, of which they are particularly fond. When food is plentiful, Coal Tits will hide it all over the place so they can return to it when times are lean.

From Bird Watching magazine (www.birdwatching.co.uk)

Bright ideas

You don't need to be a baby to use baby wipes, they are surprisingly efficient for cleaning stainless steel so always keep a pack handy. And get a good shine on your newly cleaned stainless steel by buffing up with a few drops of baby oil on some kitchen roll.

I wish I'd said that

"If he had a brain cell it would die of loneliness."
Unknown author.

Only in Britain

Raven legends

All kinds of superstition surround ravens and it's claimed they've been present at the Tower of London since the 13th century and are protected by a royal decree. Legend has it that if all of the six resident ravens were to leave the Tower it would fall and disaster would strike.

Our Tune

Finger of Suspicion – Dickie Valentine

I'll never forget the excitement of travelling to London with a group of friends to see my favourite singer, Dickie Valentine, in a Ted Heath Swing Session at the Palladium. That handsome face combined with his smooth silky voice never failed to send shivers down my spine.

Barbara Bignell, Kettering

Photo I can't throw away

My sister and I would never throw this photo away as it is the only one we have of the Grandfather we never knew. We think it was taken on his wedding day in 1889. He left his family home in 1902, leaving a wife and two small children. We never found out where he went or, after extensive searches, where he died.

Suzanne Burton, Farnborough

Recipe of the week

Italian Sausage and Bean Stew

Serves: 4
Preparation time: 10 minutes
Cooking time: 35 minutes

- ◆ 2 tbsp sunflower oil
- ◆ 8 Italian or Sicilian sausages (herbed sausages will do)
- ◆ 1 onion, peeled and finely chopped
- ◆ 2 sticks celery, trimmed and chopped
- ◆ 3 cloves garlic, peeled and finely chopped
- ◆ 1 x 400g can chopped tomatoes
- ◆ 3 sage leaves, roughly chopped
- ◆ 2 bay leaves
- ◆ 2 x 400g cans cannellini beans, drained

1 Heat the oil in a large saucepan and fry the sausages for 10 minutes, or until they are lightly brown all over. Turn down the heat and add the onion, celery and garlic and cook for a further 10 minutes, to soften but not brown.
2 Pour in the chopped tomatoes and bring the mixture to a rolling bubble. Season well and then turn down to a simmer for 10 minutes.
3 Add sage, bay leaves and cannellini beans. Stir to mix well and give the dish a final season. Simmer for a further 5 minutes to heat through the beans and serve immediately with slices of warm Ciabatta.
© Cirio, www.cirio.co.uk

Egg-cellent!

Takes 30 minutes

Your eggs will be the best dressed in town with this adorable egg cosy

You will need:

Leftover scraps of felt in different colours
Sewing thread in contrasting colours

1 Using the template (below right) cut out two pieces in the same felt for the body and then two wing shapes from a contrasting shade of felt.

2 Pin a wing to each body shape and then using the contrasting thread attach to the body.

3 Stitch an eye onto each body part, by stitching a star shape in the middle of the head, or alternatively create eyes by sewing on two small buttons.

4 Place the two pieces together so the wings are facing outwards and pin to keep in place. Sew around the chicken from the bottom right-hand corner to the bottom left-hand corner using a blanket or running stitch.

5 Make yours look extra–special by using a different colour thread to blanket stitch along the bottom edges, remembering to leave them open to create the cosy.

◆ This project is simple enough for your grandchildren to help and is a great way of using up old scraps of felt.

Homemade Gorgeous things to make with love by Ros Badger and Elspeth Thompson, published by Collins. Priced at £14.99, available nationwide or online at Amazon.co.uk.

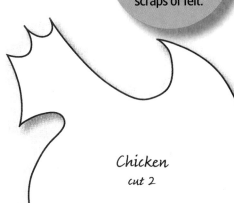

Wing
cut 2

Chicken
cut 2

◆ Enlarge template to 200% to get actual size required

Quiz of the month

Solve the answers to these well-known murder mystery questions. If you get stuck, the answers are below.

Before playing Lewis, actor Kevin Whately was a Geordie abroad

1 What was Sherlock Holmes' faithful assistant called?

2 What is Miss Marple's first name?

3 Name the Detective Chief Inspector in Midsomer Murders

4 Name the main character in the Sixties and Seventies murder mystery programme, Public Eye

5 Which century is Cadfael set in?

6 What's the first name of Agatha Christie's famous detective Poirot?

7 Name the actress who played Rosemary in Rosemary and Thyme?

8 Lewis was Inspector Morse's sidekick and is played by Kevin Whately. But in which British comedy programme did he play Neville Hope?

9 What was the name of the fictional village, which was home to Miss Marple?

10 On which island was Bergerac set ?

11 This actor is well known for playing Detective Superintendent Peter Boyd in Waking the Dead. He rose to fame by playing which character in Shoestring?

12 Which actor has been described as the definitive small screen incarnation of Sherlock Holmes?

13 Which British actor played Tom Barnaby and Detective Sergeant Jim Bergerac?

14 Name the actress who played Miss Marple and who also featured in Carry On films and Whatever Happened to the Likely Lads?

15 What is the true profession of amateur sleuths Laura Thyme and Rosemary Boxer?

16 What was Inspector Morse's first name?

17 Agatha Christie's first Poirot novel was written in 1920, but in which decade is the television series set?

ANSWERS: 1) Dr Watson 2) Jane 3) DCI John Barnaby 4) Frank Marker 5) 12th Century 6) Hercule 7) Felicity Kendal 8) Auf Wiedersehen Pet 9) St Mary Mead 10) Jersey 11) Eddie Shoestring 12) Jeremy Brett 13) John Nettles 14) Joan Hickson 15) Gardeners 16) Endeavour 17) 1930s

Fighting grime

BY: ALYSON HILBOURNE

A young policeman's lot is not a happy one...

Gloomily, Detective Constable Benson set out on his first solo case. He knew he'd been sent to investigate because everyone else thought it was a bit of a joke. Reports of washing disappearing from back gardens didn't compare with GBH or drug dealing.

"Watch your back, it's a life of grime out there!" his colleagues taunted when the Sarge assigned him the task.

The housing estate was depressing at the best of times, with boarded-up windows, old sofas dumped in gardens and wrecked cars abandoned on the roadside. He was nervous about leaving the squad car unattended as he climbed over broken children's toys to reach the door of number 17.

The huge woman who answered his knock jabbed at him with a stubby finger: "What are you lot going do about it? I can't afford to keep buying new clothes with Ronnie on benefits. That's the third shirt gone missing this week."

At number 91, an indignant old lady whined: "You can't trust anyone these days."

Looking past her into a hallway stacked with unopened boxes marked iMac, Benson agreed: "No, I suppose not."

The woman glared. "So what are you going to do?"

Benson puzzled over the answer to this. He dismissed the idea of a stakeout. The Super wasn't likely to authorise surveillance of a row of washing lines.

The answer came to him one morning as he was getting dressed. "Got it!" he yelled triumphantly, clutching a pair of new red socks to his chest. On his way to the station he stopped at number 17. He presented the large lady with his socks and persuaded her to hang them out with her own laundry.

"I don't want everyone to think I wear red socks," the woman sniffed. "It's common."

He dismissed the idea of a stakeout

"You got a better idea?" Benson asked. "Remember – no need to wash them first."

During the following week Benson cruised fruitlessly around the estate, but he searched in vain. Then on Saturday morning, just as he was giving up hope, he saw what he was looking for.

He wasn't surprised. The Dixon family were always in trouble. Artie was inside for receiving stolen goods and two of his three sons were already in youth detention. Only his wife and the baby were not inside. Benson spotted them on their way to the shops.

"This is police persecution!" Mrs Dixon howled when Benson told her to get in the car. "Just because my Artie's inside, you think you can pick on us."

"This is an entirely different matter," Benson told her through gritted teeth, as he tried to fold the buggy into the boot of his car. "I have reason to suspect you, too, and I need you to come down the station to answer some questions."

With Mrs Dixon in custody and the baby in the care of a female colleague, Benson searched her house. Most of the missing items were found. The huge woman's towels, Ronnie's shirts, and some Ann Summers underwear that Benson didn't want to imagine any of the ladies he'd met wearing, were all piled up in a bedroom at the Dixon's house. It was a fair cop,

A few weeks later, a loud voice announced: "I've come to collect my laundry."

Benson peered at the woman over the front counter. She was wearing a flowered pinny the like of which he hadn't seen since his granny died. He couldn't resist leaning a little further over to check if her stockings were, as he rightly guessed, wrinkled round her ankles.

Benson heard guffaws of laughter from his colleagues behind him, but chose to ignore them. He was relieved that someone had turned up to claim their goods. The washing had been piled up round the police station for too long.

"Get rid of it!" the sergeant had warned him.

"It's evidence, Sarge," Benson protested, but

PIC: KATE DAVIES

'What have you done to my smalls?'

that hadn't stopped his colleagues making jocular references to spin cycles and soap powders.

"So where is my laundry, then? I hope it's nice and clean," the lady in the pinny demanded. Stifled giggles could be heard from the inner office.

Benson chewed his lip. He was proud of solving this crime and hoped it would go well with the promotions board in due course, but he had a nagging suspicion that the women collecting their missing washing wouldn't be so happy.

"Through here, Madam," he said, opening a door for her. "Now what was it you wanted?" He held a clipboard with a list of items.

"Oh!" the woman screeched. "My undies!"

Benson winced. Laughter echoed along the corridor.

"They're pink!" The woman's voice was shrill with anger. "What have you done to my smalls?"

Benson tried to shrug ruefully, although he couldn't entirely suppress a smug smile. "Well, the suspect stole a pair of planted socks that I knew weren't colour-fast. And after that, I was able to track down the clothes that had turned pink in her wash…"

He didn't add that Mrs Dixon and her youngest had looked like a pair of flamingos when he'd stopped them on their way to the shops.

"These are ruined," the woman yelled, her face thunderous.

"But you've got them back," Benson pointed out, "and we've solved a crime on the estate. Helped our clean-up rate."

The woman turned to him, her fists clenched and a nasty glint in her eye.

"Clean-up rate, is it, laddie?" she repeated, swinging a pink pair of knickers at him. "You call this clean?"

Benson backed slowly out of the room, arms outstretched in what he hoped was a calming gesture. "Madam, please don't do anything you might regret. It's just a bit of dye. I'm sure it will all come out in the wash…"

Thursday

1

All Saints' Day

Friday

2

Saturday

3

Sunday

4

Monday

5

Guy Fawkes' Night

Tuesday

6

Wednesday

7

Thursday

8

Friday

9

Saturday

10

Sunday

11

Remembrance Sunday

Monday

12

Tuesday

13

Wednesday

14

Thursday

15

Friday

16

Saturday

17

Sunday

18

Monday

19

Tuesday

20

Wednesday

21

Thursday

22

Friday **23**	Tuesday **27**
Saturday **24**	Wednesday **28**
Sunday **25**	Thursday **29**
Monday **26**	Friday **30** *St Andrew's Day (Bank Holiday Scotland)*

PIC: ISTOCKPHOTO

Poem of the month

Winter draws on

Take me big coat out the closet,
Me thermal undies out the drawer.
No more sun-tops or bikinis,
Winter's knocking on the door.

Out come me scarf and gloves,
Me old faithful woolly hat
That kept me warm last year
(And the year before that).

They're not the height of fashion
But they will have to do
'Cos I ain't got the readies
To buy everything brand new.

But me poor old boots have had it,
I'll just have to buy a pair.
Last year I used a cornflakes box
To make a new insole.

I thought I was very clever
Thus bunging up the hole,
But found I'd soggy cardboard
Underneath me feet,
As it turned to papier mâché
When I walked along the street.
Mrs J G Vicente, Romford, Essex

My Teenage Years
'A pony tail a-hanging down'

When I was 13 we only had BBC television so if I wanted to watch Oh Boy! on ITV, I had to go round to my friend's house. There was a young singer on the programme called Cliff Richard who I thought was great. When he came to the Guildford Odeon in March 1959, I was there – and again in September when it was announced that his backing group had changed their name from The Drifters to The Shadows.

In those days, I was a regular 'pony-tailed teenager' and went to as many pop concerts as I could. I saw Tommy Steele at the Winter Gardens in Bournemouth when I was staying with my Grandmother. I remember seeing Jimmy Tarbuck outside the Odeon theatre gates at the end of a show. He didn't have a pen to sign autographs so he borrowed mine. When he returned it, he squeezed my hand and said thank you. After that, I always had a soft spot for him.

Pamela enjoyed watching her pop idols perform live

Sometimes when my friends and I had been to the first show of the evening, we'd see that the fire door was ajar so we used to creep in after the second show had started and watch it all over again from the balcony for free.

I met my future husband when we were both working for the borough council. He wrote his extension number in a Valentine card he sent to my office. We married when I was 20.

Pamela Patten, Portugal

Bird of the week

PIC: ISTOCK

Greenfinch

A well-known visitor to gardens, the Greenfinch will nest in a conifer and feed on black sunflower seeds if it gets the chance. So fond are they of this particular seed that they will fling other seeds aside in a mixed feeder to get at the favoured titbits. Outside the breeding season they can often be found in large flocks, occupying most of the UK all year, apart from the north of Scotland and its islands which they visit only in summer.
From Bird Watching magazine (www.birdwatching.co.uk)

Bright ideas

Mark your front door key with a little luminous paint to distinguish it from the others on the key ring. This will save time fumbling in the dark, and prove a good safety measure, as you'll get into the house quicker.
From Mrs Chambers, Hammersmith, London

I wish I'd said that

"He has no enemies, but is intensely disliked by his friends." **Oscar Wilde on an anonymous subject.**

Only in Britain

Tall tales

Years ago a Wasdale Valley publican would enthral his punters with tall tales. Now, in his memory, an annual competition takes place to find the biggest liar. One past competitor triumphed simply with the claim, 'I've never told a lie in my life'!

Our Tune

Portrait Of My Love – Matt Monro

Aged 16 I took a weekend job at a motorway service station. One weekend I was clearing tables when in walked Matt Monro! I told him 'Portrait of My Love' had really changed my way of looking at music. He thanked me, took my hand and sang it to me.

Mrs E Booker, Sutton-in-Ashfield, Notts

Photo I can't throw away

This photo always brings a smile to my face. It portrays friendship in the rain. All three of us friends (I'm in the middle) were 18 at the time and looking forward to the future. Even though it was raining, you can see we were a happy bunch. We lost touch with Jean but Anne and myself remain lifelong friends, both in our 70s now.

Doreen Leonard, Mill Hill, London

Recipe of the week

Cookie Crumble Cheesecake

Serves: 6-8
Preparation time: 15 minutes
Chilling time: 1 hour

◆ 175g digestive biscuits
◆ 275g Galaxy Cookie Crumble chocolate
◆ 300g cream cheese
◆ 200g double cream
◆ 2 tsp lime juice
◆ 50g caster sugar

To serve:
◆ Galaxy Cookie Crumble chocolate shavings

1 Lightly grease a 20cm (8in) loose-bottomed flan or tart tin.
2 Place the digestive biscuits in a large bowl and bash with the end of a rolling pin, until they are randomly broken, with some chunks and crumbs.
3 Melt 125g of the chocolate in a bowl over a pan of simmering water. Then stir this into the biscuits and mix well, to coat all the crumbs with chocolate.
4 Pour the mixture into the tart tin and press down evenly with the back of a spoon. Place the tin in the fridge for at least 30 minutes.
5 Meanwhile, melt the remaining chocolate. In a mixing bowl, beat together the cream cheese, cream, lime juice and sugar. Pour in the melted chocolate and stir a little bit, but not enough to mix it in completely.
6 Spoon this onto the biscuit base and smooth over very roughly. Chill for another half hour at least. Just before serving decorate with the shavings of chocolate.

◆ **Top tip:** If you can't find this particular chocolate bar replace with chocolate covered digestives, use your favourite chocolate and decorate with broken Maltesers.
© Galaxy, www.galaxychocolate.co.uk

My Teenage Years
The clerk's tale

I had a wonderful start in life as my first job was on the switchboard in a solicitor's office. I was soon given the job of articled clerk which was very varied and gave me a lot of responsibility.

Many of my tasks took me to London and I became familiar with the barristers' chambers in Lincoln's Inn Fields, the Law Courts, the Inland Revenue and Somerset House. Part of my job was to make payments at these different places so my briefcase often contained a great deal of money.

One day when I was walking across the courtyard of Somerset House, I opened my bag to see what was next on my list and all the loose pound notes flew out over the courtyard. Passers-by rushed around, picking them up for me. People were very honest in those days – I wasn't short by even one pound.

When I was told that I would be going to 'the bear garden', I was intrigued and rather scared – until

Margaret aged 16

I found out that it was the name given to a place in the Law Courts where solicitors, barristers and mere clerks like myself met. I always enjoyed the atmosphere there.

Going to Lincoln's Inn Fields was like stepping into another world with all the barristers walking around carrying the blue bags containing their briefs. The bags were blue because there was a king on the throne – these days the bags are pink as we have a queen.

Margaret Lavender, Boston, Lincs

Bird of the week

Grey Wagtail

PIC: ISTOCK

Misleadingly named, the Grey Wagtail's most noticeable colour is yellow. Not to be confused with the Yellow Wagtail, a summer-only visitor, the Grey is with us all year, although it moves in winter from upland areas to lowland. They often come to gardens, but usually only if there's a pond because they eat insects that are found around water. They're also partial to water snails and tadpoles if the water is shallow enough to get at them.

From Bird Watching magazine (www.birdwatching.co.uk)

Bright ideas

For the best tasting soups and stews, add salt gradually throughout the cooking process. This gives the salt time to disperse and interact with the molecules of food to give it deeper subtle flavouring.

I wish I'd said that

"If men can run the world, why can't they stop wearing neckties? How intelligent is it to start the day by tying a little noose around your neck?'
Linda Ellerbee, American journalist

Only in Britain

Remember, remember

Bonfire night celebrations and the story of Guy Fawkes is revived every November 5th, but certain parts of England take it all very seriously. Lewes, for example, has seven bonfire societies, which, between them, cover different areas of the town to make it easier for more locals to enjoy the celebrations.

Our Tune

Love Is A Many Splendored Thing – The Four Aces

In 1955 my husband and I had our first date, seeing 'Love Is a Many Splendored Thing', which was set in Hong Kong and showed many places Maurice had served with the RAOC. It is still our tune, and we have proven that love really is a many splendored thing.

Mrs E Walton, Halesowen, West Midlands

Photo I can't throw away

This is a photograph of the 1966 Preliminary Training School at Broadgreen Hospital in Liverpool. It was taken at the beginning of our nurse training, which was hard and tiring work but so rewarding. It was a solid foundation and the springboard of many long and successful careers in health, both at home and abroad. Many of those in the snapshot have met at ten-year milestones since we finished. Our last was the 40-year reunion in 2008.   **Anne Jones, Preston**

Recipe of the week

Beef and Mushroom Spaghetti

Serves: 4
Preparation time: 10 minutes
Cooking time: 25–30 minutes

◆ 1 tbsp olive oil
◆ 500g lean beef mince
◆ 1 onion, chopped
◆ 1–2 cloves garlic, crushed
◆ 350g closed cup mushrooms, halved
◆ 150ml (6 fl oz) red wine
◆ 400g can chopped tomatoes
◆ 1 tsp dried oregano
◆ 1 bay leaf
◆ 1 tbsp tomato puree
◆ 300ml (12 fl oz) beef or vegetable stock
◆ 400g dried spaghetti, to serve

1 Heat the oil in a large heavy-bottomed saucepan. Add the mince and onion and sauté over a high heat for 5 minutes, or until the mince is lightly browned. Then add the garlic and mushrooms and sauté for a further 5 minutes.
2 Add the remaining ingredients and season to taste. Bring to the boil, cover and simmer for 20 minutes or until the mushrooms are tender and the sauce has thickened. Remove the lid halfway through cooking so the sauce can thicken.
3 Meanwhile, cook the pasta in a large saucepan of boiling, salted water according to the packet instructions. When the meat sauce is ready, remove the bay leaf and season as necessary. Serve with the freshly cooked spaghetti.

◆ **Top tip:** This tastes even better the next day so keep those leftovers.
© The Mushroom Bureau, www.mushroomsmakesense.com

My Teenage Years
The Stones rolled in

I was born and raised in Ramsgate. It was a two-hour train journey to the bright lights of London so instead we teenagers headed for the neon-lit sea front of Margate. There we sampled the sticky cocktail delights of the Kon Tiki bar and danced at the Dreamland ballroom (screaming loudly at the groups who had ventured down to play in venues on the south-east coast).

Enter my Dad, who used to be a professional footballer. In the Fifties he had started a football team which by the Sixties had expanded into the Ramsgate Sporting Youth Club. When he realised that the town's youngsters were travelling to Margate for their weekend entertainment he instigated dances at the rarely used Westcliff Hall, which was actually built in to the chalk cliff.

Some of the top groups of the era played there, including The Kinks and The Swinging Blue Jeans, and I still have the posters advertising those gigs. But THE event of the year for us was when The Rolling Stones came to our little seaside town. No advertising was needed, word-of-mouth was enough – I sold

Linda (right) in her best C&A outfit circa 1965

tickets at school for 10s each.

Sadly, our dances didn't last very long as the town council deemed the Westcliff Hall to be unsafe for dancing. The teenagers of Ramsgate revolted – we marched on the town hall with placards proclaiming 'Save Our Dances', but to no avail. The council stopped the dances and closed the hall (which in fact is still standing today).

Linda Plant, Hitchin, Herts

Bird of the week

PIC: ISTOCK

Siskin

Nomadic by nature you're unlikely to see the same Siskin in your garden two years running. Although they stay in roughly the same area, they roam around, and in winter our local bird numbers are swollen by visitors from Germany and Scandinavia. They feed on the seeds of birch, alder, spruce and pine, but they are particularly drawn to red seed holders in gardens, for reasons unknown. So to attract these pretty yellow finches, invest in red feeders!

From Bird Watching magazine (www.birdwatching.co.uk)

Bright ideas

When a recipe calls for egg yolks, freeze the remaining egg whites in an ice-cube tray, taking care to put one egg white in each ice cube section. This way, when you need, for example, three egg whites, pop three out, leave to defrost to room temperature and use as normal.

I wish I'd said that

"I'm not offended by all the dumb blonde jokes because I know I'm not dumb... and I also know that I'm not blonde." **Dolly Parton**

Only in Britain
Pussy cat tales

Cats are unfortunate enough to be included in superstitions around the world, making them lucky or unlucky depending where you're from. In Scotland a strange black cat on your porch predicts prosperity, while in the 16th century visitors were encouraged to kiss the family cat on arrival!

Our Tune
I Got You Babe – Sonny and Cher

My husband and I have been married for more than 40 years. We cleared a dance floor together at Rye Pier on the Isle of Wight when I was 16 singing and dancing to this tune. Even now, we still sing at the top of our voices whenever we hear it.

Judy Freeman, Peterborough

Photo I can't throw away

I love this photo of me and my brother, Neil, in our double pushchair with Mum standing behind. It was taken in 1967 outside the house where we were both born in Chalk, Kent. Mum says she had been shopping in the village and we had both fallen asleep on the way home. She thought we looked so cute together she asked Dad to take a picture. I love how it shows a snapshot of life in the Sixties.

Amanda Whitworth, Norwich

Recipe of the week

Turkey and Cranberry Biryani

Serves: 4
Preparation time: 20-25 minutes
Cooking time: 15-20 minutes

- ◆ 10cm (4 inch) piece cucumber, diced
- ◆ Small handful fresh coriander
- ◆ 6 tbsp natural yogurt
- ◆ 350g basmati rice
- ◆ 1 tsp salt
- ◆ 2 tbsp vegetable oil
- ◆ 1 large onion, finely chopped
- ◆ 1 red chilli, deseeded and finely chopped
- ◆ 2 tsp each of minced garlic and ginger
- ◆ 1 tsp each of ground coriander and turmeric
- ◆ 2 tsp ground cumin
- ◆ 3 carrots, cut into small chunks
- ◆ 225g cooked turkey
- ◆ 300ml (12 fl oz) hot chicken stock
- ◆ 3 tbsp chunky cranberry sauce
- ◆ 1 tsp garam masala
- ◆ Juice of 1 lemon
- ◆ 175g French beans, trimmed

1 Make a raita by mixing together the cucumber, coriander and natural yogurt and season to taste. Chill until you're ready to serve.

2 Wash the rice and put into a medium saucepan with 600ml (1 pint) cold water and a pinch of salt. Bring to the boil, then simmer for 10 minutes, or until just tender and all the water has been absorbed. Remove from the heat, cover and set aside.

3 Meanwhile, heat the oil in a large frying pan and fry the onion, chilli, garlic, ginger, spices and carrots for 5-6 minutes, stirring frequently. Add the turkey and stock and simmer for 5-6 minutes. Stir in the cranberry sauce, garam masala, lemon juice and beans. Cover and simmer for 5 minutes, or until the stock reduces and the beans are tender.

4 Fluff up the rice with a fork and stir into the vegetable mixture. Serve with a dollop of the raita and poppadoms.

© Ocean Spray, www.oceanspray.co.uk

My Teenage Years
'Rebel, rebel'

If you've got the legs for hotpants, then flaunt it like Joy

I packed many 'firsts' into my teenage years. First love, first broken heart, first job and leaving home. If I was going to change the world, 17 seemed a good time to start.

How naïve I was. I'd never had 'the chat' with Mum so how I avoided her warning 'not to bring trouble home', I'll never know, because I had no idea what she meant.

I moved in to 'digs' with a kind, retired lady – but when I found her filling the kettle from my cold hot water bottle and she loomed up from behind the aspidistra as I crept in one night (checking to see if I'd brought a boyfriend home), it was time to move on.

To Mum's horror, I got a bedsit. Sharing a kitchen and a fungus-dotted bathroom helped my seven guineas a week stretch to independent living. I learned to budget, ate from Fine Fare's reduced counter, saved a little, and had money to spend on clothes (like hot pants) and music (loud) of which my parents disapproved.

Regrets? A few, but I learned from them and believe they made me stronger and shaped the grown-up I became. This was my small but sweet rebellion, recounted with edited highlights at weekends when it took me two hours by bus and train to go home for one of Mum's much-missed Sunday roasts.

By the end of my 20s, I'd be married with my first mortgage and first baby. Happy, but never again so carefree as in my teenage years.

Joy Harris, Peterborough

Bird of the week

PIC: ISTOCK

Jackdaw

These inquisitive and intelligent black birds with their distinctive dark grey heads, Jackdaws are increasingly being seen in British gardens. One of the Corvid family of birds that includes Crows, Rooks, Magpies and Jays, Jackdaw's get their name from the tchak sound of their calls. Although they have a reputation for being cruel birds, perhaps because their very varied diet includes the eggs of other birds, they are actually very sociable and will share their food with siblings to ensure the survival of all.
From Bird Watching magazine (www.birdwatching.co.uk)

Bright ideas

Know your onions! For dishes that require long slivers for decoration, like French onion soup, slice them lengthways for pretty strips. If you want speed of cooking or as an ingredient to add bulk to a sauce, chop them finely crossways.

I wish I'd said that

Bernard Shaw invited Winston Churchill to the first night of a new play and ended with the cutting line: "Bring a friend – if you have one." **Churchill's reply:** "Impossible to be present for the first performance. Will attend the second – if there is one."

Only in Britain

Time for tea

We're a nation of tea lovers, so it isn't surprising there are a few superstitions surrounding our favourite cuppa. It was once considered bad luck for more than one female to pour from the same teapot and also leaving the lid off while brewing meant a visit from a stranger.

Our Tune

Unchained Melody – Jimmy Young

Back in 1957 I was a TB patient at the Royal Seabathing Hospital in Margate. I was engaged to be married and my father thought my future husband would abandon me. He didn't, and we were married for 51 years. The words of this song mean so much to me.

Marion Kirby, Canterbury

Photo I can't throw away

Here is a lovely photograph of my Gran, Emily Simmons – a photo which I cannot throw away. It was taken in 1939 on the day of my christening. I remember she was always smartly dressed, as you can see in the picture. I was the first grandchild in the family, so as you can imagine I was quite spoiled! Gran passed away when I was quite young, so I treasure this photo of her now.

Valerie Thomas, Wrexham, Clwyd

Pina Colada

Serves 2
Preparation time: 10 minutes

◆ 3 tbsp white rum
◆ 100ml (4 fl oz) reduced-fat coconut milk
◆ 150ml (6 fl oz) fresh pineapple juice
◆ 5 tsp granulated sweetener
◆ 4-5 crushed ice cubes
To decorate:
◆ 2 pieces of fresh pineapple (canned will do)
◆ 2 glace cherries

1 Put all the ingredients into a cocktail shaker and shake until combined. If you haven't got a cocktail shaker then an empty 2-litre water bottle will do.
2 Pour into two glasses and decorate by putting a piece of pineapple and cherry on a cocktail stick and balance this across the glasses

◆ **Top tip:** Simply leave out the rum to make this a fun non-alcoholic party drink. You can also replace the sweetener with normal caster sugar if you wish.
© Canderel, www.canderel.co.uk

My Teenage Years
Mamma mia

I used to be sent to the café round the corner to buy the family's weekly treat, a bowl of ice cream. I took our own container to hold the scoops of vanilla topped with raspberry sauce. When I was 13, the café's owner, Mrs DeMarco, asked if I would like to work for her. I thought all my Christmases had come at once and I skipped home to tell my mother the good news.

The shop had a specially converted glass-topped counter in which the ice-cream could be seen freshly churning. There were wooden benches (not very comfortable) for customers to sit on. I worked there for two years, rushing home after school to have my evening meal first. For a 40-hour week, I earned 12s 6d.

As well as ice-cream, we sold sweets by the quarter pound – toffees, liquorice allsorts, jelly babies and mint humbugs. At weekends, shoppers came in for lunch. In the evenings, teenagers congregated to drink hot orange, lemon or chocolate and the juke-box played non-stop. This was my

At the age of 13 Helen landed her dream job

favourite time of the day and the dulcet tones of Ray Charles still transport me back to the Sixties.

Mrs DeMarco was like a second mother to me, making sure my school work did not suffer. Between customers, I sat at the kitchen table to do my homework with her children. She was a role model who taught me something of the Italian language and cuisine, and general day-to-day life.

Helen Minto, Berwickshire

Bird of the week

PIC: ISTOCK

Goldcrest

This is the UK's smallest bird, the Goldcrest even beats the tiny Wren to the crown. For a bird that is relatively hard to see, there are far more than you might imagine. Our resident birds number 800,000 but winter migrants from Europe swell that number to something approaching 5 million. Conifer plantations, particularly along the east and south coasts of England, are the places to be in winter to catch a flash of bright orange on the heads of these little birds, flitting among the foliage.
From Bird Watching magazine (www.birdwatching.co.uk)

Bright ideas

Do you spend an age trying to find the end of a roll of sellotape? Simply stick a small button at the end, or fold it over so it sticks to itself and you'll never have a problem again. Particularly useful when you have lots of presents to wrap!

I wish I'd said that

"Behind every successful man is a surprised woman."
Maryon Pearson, wife of Canada's 14th Prime Minister.

Only in Britain

Muddy good fun

What could be more barmy than racing through mud? It's hilarious to watch and the event, that takes place in Maldon, Essex, has raised lots of money for charity. Competitors of all ages take part as they scrabble, sprint or flounder through thick mud! **To find out about the next event visit www.maldonmudrace.com.**

Our Tune

Underneath the Arches – Flanagan and Allen

Recently, we had a Thanksgiving Service for my husband, Peter. As people arrived at the church, the organist played some of his favourite tunes. The Rector started the service by saying: "I've never walked down the aisle to the tune of 'Underneath the Arches' before!" It made us all smile.

Sheila Sorrell, Bradenham, Norfolk

Photo I can't throw away

I thought I would send you a picture of my first husband and I, taken while he was on leave after our son had been born. It's the hat that makes me laugh – to think we wore hats at 19! Those were the days when it was hats and gloves or you were not dressed up. We both married again and were happy in our new relationships. Sadly neither one is now with us, but life goes on.

Doris Glasby, Malton, North Yorkshire

Recipe of the week

Chocolate and Amaretto Panna Cotta

Serves 6
Preparation time: 15 minutes
Cooking time: 15 minutes (plus 6 hours, or overnight chilling)

◆ 1 tbsp powdered gelatine
◆ 175g dark chocolate, chopped
◆ 225ml (9 fl oz) organic whole milk
◆ 4 tbsp caster sugar
◆ 4 tbsp Amaretto
◆ 325g organic natural yogurt

To decorate:
◆ Dark chocolate curls
◆ Fresh berries

1 Brush six 150ml (6 fl oz) pudding bowls or ramekins with a little sunflower oil. Place 4 tablespoons of the milk in a small saucepan and sprinkle over the powdered gelatine. Leave to stand for 5 minutes.
2 In another small saucepan, combine the remaining milk, sugar and chocolate and melt over a low heat, stirring frequently.
3 Dissolve the gelatine over a low heat but do not allow it to boil. Then pour this into the chocolate milk and whisk to combine. Leave the mixture to cool to room temperature before whisking in the Amaretto and yogurt.
4 Pour the mixture into the prepared dishes and cover. Chill for at least 6 hours, or preferably overnight. Make the chocolate curls by peeling strands off a bar of dark chocolate using a vegetable peeler or sharp knife.
5 To serve, loosen the puddings by sliding a knife around the edges. Invert onto a plate and tap firmly, they should come unstuck. Decorate the tops of the panna cotta with the curls of dark chocolate and a couple of fresh berries on each plate.

© Yeo Valley Organic, www.yeovalleyorganic.co.uk

Brilliant bracelets

Make your own bracelet in four easy steps

Takes 30 minutes

You will need:

10cm (4 inch) of fine silver chain
2 x silver rings with two eyes (loops either side)
4 x 6mm faceted beads
1 x large glass bead
2 x 14mm silver bead caps
2 x 4mm crystal half-silver faceted glass beads
4 x silver headpins (wire with nail like head on one end)
1 x silver eye pin
1 x 7mm spring ring fastening
Flat-nosed pliers
Half round-nosed pliers
Wire cutters

1 Thread an eye pin with a crystal faceted bead, a bead cap, your large glass bead, then another bead cap and crystal faceted bead.

2 Using flat-nosed pliers bend the end of the pin to a right angle and then cut, leaving 1cm (¼inch) of wire above the bead. Bend the pin into a loop using the round-nosed pliers.

3 Thread two headpins through the inside of a silver ring then thread a larger coloured faceted bead on to each side. Bend one end of the headpin and cut before threading on half of the fine chain and bending into a loop to secure it to the chain. Attach the other pin to the assembled large central bead. Repeat this process to the other side of the central bead.

4 Attach the spring-fastening components by opening the end links of the chain. Check all your loops are secure before wearing.

◆ **Choose different coloured beads and add charms to create an entirely different look.**

Bracelets (£4.99) by Amanda Walker and published by Search Press is part of the Twenty to make easy craft series, call 01892 510850 or visit www.searchpress.com

Quiz of the month

Can you match the following characters to their well-known television programmes? If you get stuck the answers are below.

The cast of Bonanza – but what was the name of Lorne Green's character?

1 Bonanza
2 Dr Finlay's Casebook
3 All Creatures Great and Small
4 The Saint
5 Six Million Dollar Man
6 The Persuaders!
7 The Professionals
8 General Hospital
9 Danger Man
10 The Man From Laramie
11 Secret Army
12 Soldier Soldier
13 When the Boat Comes In
14 Z-Cars
15 Absolutely Fabulous
16 Jewel in the Crown
17 Keeping up Appearances
18 Lovejoy
19 Minder
20 Yes, Minister

A Ben Cartwright
B Inspector Teal
C Jack Ford
D Albert Foiret
E George Cowley
F Will Lockhart
G Hari Kumar
H Dr Neville Bywaters
I Tinker
J Steve Austin
K Hyacinth Bucket
L Edina Monsoon
M Seigfried Farnon
N Terry McCann
O DCI Charlie Barlow
P Danny Wilde
Q Sir Humphrey Appleby
R Fusilier Dave Tucker
S Dr Angus Cameron
T Secret Agent John Drake

ANSWERS: 1) A 2) S 3) M 4) B 5) J 6) P 7) E 8) H 9) T 10) F 11) D 12) R 13) C 14) O 15) L 16) G 17) K 18) I 19) N 20) Q

Nanny knew best

BY: DANNIE NICHOLAS

One Christmas present remains etched in Mike's memory...

Christmas 1955 affected my seven-year-old mind so deeply that I still remember every moment. It began happily enough. We were to spend Christmas, as usual, at the farm where my grandfather was foreman. There would be 19 of us with my mum's sisters and their families.

On Christmas Eve, we set off in Dad's old Ford for Bean Bottom Farm. Dad unloaded everything, then chugged away into the darkness. He was on the late shift at the sugar beet factory so had to work through the night.

I stepped into the bright hall, which was about the size of our council flat. As always, I hurried first to greet the stuffed golden pheasant in his glass case. A plaque explained when and where it had been shot but as I couldn't read this meant nothing to me. I hated even trying to read...

Next, I peeked into Nanny's front room. Every square inch was covered with cakes, meats, fruit and presents. "Outta there, boy!" My nanny rumbled towards me, built like a Churchill tank but ever ready to dissolve into girlish giggles. "No sneaking about, young Michael! Straight up to bed with you, lest Father Christmas don't come!"

In the lamp-lit bedroom, shared with my cousins Matt and Joe, I gazed out into the darkness of the black fen while Mum searched out my pyjamas. "Into bed and off to sleep straight away!"

Early next day, I crept downstairs to the kitchen where a turkey was already roasting in the huge black range. But what took my interest was the three piles of presents; two for my cousins, the third for me.

"Go on, Mike!" said my weary dad, just back from work and bound soon for bed. "Let's see what Father Christmas brought you!" Mum was perched on the arm of his chair, her arm around his shoulder.

But this was a pleasure not to be spoiled by

'Let's see what Father Christmas brought you'

hurrying. I knew exactly what I wanted to be inside the biggest parcel. Being an avid Wild West fan, I'd asked Father Christmas for the silver-plated Colt .45 I'd seen in a Norwich toyshop. My reverie was broken by the noisy arrival of Matt and Joe. They charged across the kitchen and began ripping open presents. Both pulled out toy Winchester 73 rifles and began to massacre imaginary redskins.

I unwrapped my presents, starting with the smallest and working my way up – at last – to that big parcel. But it was not my beloved Colt .45. It was a toy typewriter. A red thing with a custard-yellow dial that you turned to get the letter you wanted to type, then thumped to print it.

I could barely write so why did I need a stupid typewriter?

I looked up at Mum and Dad. They smiled expectantly. I tried to smile back. But I failed and began to cry instead. "Father Christmas made a mistake!" I howled. My Dad rose and left, presumably to go to bed, picking up a bottle as he went. Mum began clearing away discarded wrapping paper, not saying a word.

My cousins grabbed my arms and dragged me out into the hall. Joe whispered: "Want to know a secret, Mike?"

In my misery, I could not care less.

"There ain't no Father Christmas! Your Mum and Dad got you that typewriter, see, not no bloody Father Christmas making a mistake!"

I felt betrayed. First, by my cousins telling me there was no Father Christmas and, secondly, by my parents giving me an 'educational toy' because I was a failure at school. I began to howl again. Mum rushed out of the kitchen. "What you two doin' to Mike?" she demanded. Matt and Joe fled.

"Come here, sweetheart," Mum whispered.

I turned to run, but was halted by the sight of Dad. He hadn't gone to bed, after all. He was sitting on the step at the open front door, taking gulps from his bottle and giggling at the falling snow. Mum

'Come on and show me how this gadget works'

shoved me into the kitchen and slammed the door behind me. Then I heard her and Dad shouting, something I'd never heard in my life before.

"Come on and show me how this gadget of yours works," said my Nanny. She thrust me down at the table and plonked the typewriter in front of me – and wouldn't leave until I'd started to bang away at it.

So bang away I did. As violently as I could. Nanny reappeared at my shoulder. She ripped out the paper I'd covered in gobbledegook and inserted a clean sheet. "Enough of that squit! Type your name, boy." I'd never heard my Nanny use that tone before.

"Type your bloody name!" she boomed. Mum and Dad stopped arguing. Even the wind fell silent. I began typing. After three attempts, my name appeared. The Churchill tank wrapped me in a smothering hug. "Now type everyone's name," she ordered.

Everyone's name?

"Then you can cut them out, see, and we can use 'em for nameplates on the dinner table. Seen 'em when I were in service. Won't it be grand!" She stared down at me, staring up at her. "Come on, don't just sit there blinking!"

So I banged away while Nanny and my aunties cooked the dinner and my Mum and Dad got merrily tipsy together, watching the snowflakes flutter down.

I still have that typewriter, along with the pair of spectacles that Nanny discovered I needed, displayed in the hall next to the golden pheasant. I own Bean Bottom Farm now, you see. And I make a very good living – writing cowboy stories.

December 2012

Saturday

1

Sunday

2

Monday

3

Tuesday

4

Wednesday

5

Thursday

6

Friday

7

Saturday

8

Sunday

9

Monday

10

Tuesday

11

Wednesday

12

Thursday

13

Friday

14

Saturday

15

Sunday

16

Monday

17

Tuesday

18

Wednesday

19

Thursday

20

Friday

21

Shortest Day (Winter Solstice)

Saturday

22

Sunday	Friday
23	**28**
Monday	Saturday
24 *Christmas Eve*	**29**
Tuesday	Sunday
25 *Christmas Day*	**30**
Wednesday	Monday
26 *Boxing Day*	**31** *New Year's Eve/ Hogmanay*
Thursday	
27	

Poem of the month

The Christmas message

Once more the bells are ringing,
Their message loud and clear.
And postmen bring us Christmas cards
From loved ones, far and near.

We rush to buy Christmas presents,
The food, the beer, the sherry,
Looking forward to time off work
When we can all be merry.

And all the little children
Can't wait for Santa Claus
To come down sooty chimneys,
Or open locked front doors!

But at this lovely Christmastime,
How many will remember
What it's really all about,
The twenty-fifth of December?

Peace and love to all mankind,
The message is loud and clear,
To love and cherish everyone,
Be they strangers, or those most dear.
**Doreen Williams,
Halesowen, W Midlands**

My Teenage Years
Rookie reporter

I had wanted to become a journalist after my English teacher suggested this would be the right career for me, but I hadn't envisaged the unusual way I landed my first job. My mother was working in a sweet shop when a reporter from the local paper popped in to ask if she had any stories. She didn't, but when she saw his van starting up, she ran after him. His eyes lit up. "Have you got a story, after all?" he asked. "No," she replied. "But I do have a daughter who wants to become a reporter."

Five days later, the editor, Mr Collicutt, offered me a job and at the age of 18 I became a trainee on the Wiltshire and Gloucestershire Standard, affectionately known as the Hedge and Ditcher. "Your first assignment," he told me, "is to cover a visit by the Queen Mother and her meeting with a pelican!"

Pesky pelican was a challenge for this cub reporter

It turned out that the Queen Mother was president-in-chief of RAF Little Rissington, then home to the Red Arrows display team. As you'd expect, the Queen Mother behaved immaculately but I wish I could say the same about the pelican! This particular mascot had a mind of its own and seemed particularly keen on anything shiny, including buttons on uniforms and the tip of my pen for which it made an unsuccessful lunge.

Fortunately, I returned to the office in one piece in time to pen my first front-page report. It was a proud moment.

Rita Sobot (by email)

Bird of the week

PIC: ISTOCK

Sparrowhawk

Many people curse the Sparrowhawk because of its tendency to take small birds off our feeders in a snatch-and-grab raid. But look closely and it is revealed to be the most beautiful of birds and a handy indicator of the health of the local songbird population. The old adage goes that prey controls predators, not the other way around. Ie, in areas where there are few small birds, you will not find Sparrowhawks, so the sight of one should be a glad one.

From Bird Watching magazine (www.birdwatching.co.uk)

Bright ideas

If you always find getting scrambled eggs or cheese sauce off your saucepans tricky, it's due to hot water further sticking the culprits onto the pan. So as soon as you finish, give the pan a rinse in cold water to cool it down, before washing as normal.

I wish I'd said that

"I've only got one nerve left, and you're getting on it."

Only in Britain

Festive frolics

Want to burn some extra calories then compete in one of the charity Christmas pudding races taking place this December across the country. Most are yuletide themed fancy dress, so expect to see sprinting crackers, jogging elves and reluctant reindeer doing their bit for charity.

Our Tune

I'll Be Loving You Always – Frank Sinatra

For the first year of our marriage in 1947, my husband was posted to Singapore. This song was mentioned in letters to one another during this time. It remained in the background until our 40th anniversary, when my husband's gift to me was accompanied by the words of the song. **P B Watson, Blackpool**

Photo I can't throw away

This is a picture of my lovely Dad, me, and my new little bear, Fred, on a trip down the Thames in about 1934. Dad loved to take me on adventures, and this was one of them. We had great fun, as we always did. Dad was Scottish, and we moved there when war broke out, but I have very fond memories of our time living in London. And, after several makeovers, Fred the bear still sits on my bedside table now!
Anne Saunders, Great Yarmouth, Norfolk

Recipe of the week

Cranberry Mince Pies

Makes: 20
Preparation time: 20 minutes (plus 10 minutes chilling)
Cooking time: 15–20 minutes

For the mincemeat:
◆ 100g sweetened dried cranberries
◆ 1 x 400g jar mincemeat
◆ 25g chopped almonds

For the pastry:
◆ 500g plain flour
◆ 2 tbsp icing sugar
◆ 250g butter, diced and at room temperature
◆ Icing sugar, for dusting

1 Grease a cupcake baking tin (enough to hold 20 pies). Using a small saucepan, cover the cranberries with water and bring to the boil. Then reduce the heat and simmer for 10 minutes. Set aside to cool.
2 Meanwhile, preheat the oven to 180°C/350°F.Gas Mark 4. In a large mixing bowl, sift in the flour and icing sugar. Add the butter and, using your fingertips, gently rub it in until the mixture resembles fine breadcrumbs. Add 6–7 tablespoons of cold water until you have a soft dough. Wrap this in polythene film and chill for 10 minutes.
3 Meanwhile drain any excess liquid from the cranberries before mixing it into the mincemeat and chopped almonds.
4 Roll the pastry to approximately 3mm (1/8 inch) thickness and using an 7½ cm (3 inch) cutter, make 20 rounds and put into the prepared baking tin. Spoon approximately 1 tablespoons of the mincemeat into each case. Use the leftover pastry to cut strips to form the lattice topping. Bake for 15–20 minutes, or until golden.
© Ocean Spray, www.oceanspray.co.uk

My Teenage Years
Dear diary

I still have my teenage diary for those years so I remember very well what I was doing in the Fifties. I lived in Chingford and went to Walthamstow High School for Girls from 1953 to 1958. From the beginning, I was into rock 'n' roll music and was lucky enough to see Bill Hayley in Edmonton in 1957. It was even more exciting to see Buddy Holly in March 1958.

I also loved the clothes of that era – the full skirts with lots of petticoats, sometimes even hoops, underneath. I wanted to be a dress designer so embarked on an apprenticeship at Lachasse couture house in Mayfair. I attended evening classes for pattern cutting and design at St Martin's School of Art. I also used to go to some of the well-known coffee bars of that era, Heaven and Hell and the 2i's.

I went to Germany for six weeks to stay with a penfriend. It was quite a change for a city girl to

Kay in June 1957 wearing a wonderful Fifties outfit

stay on a farm and, as it was not long after the war, I felt that I had to be an ambassador for my country, despite not speaking the language.

Before I met the man who has been my husband for more than 50 years, I had crush on a boy who lived across the road from us. He was at the grammar school and just to see him coming home from school on his bike was enough in those days.

Kay Barrett, North Hykeham, Lincs

Bird of the week

PIC: ISTOCK

Treecreeper

The little Treecreeper is a prime example of specialism. It makes its living by walking up the trunks of trees, probing the bark for insects and spiders. To do this it has long, agile toes, a downward curving, thin beak and a stiff tail that braces it against the tree. The male and female both build their nest behind loose bark using twigs, moss and dried grass, with a feather lining. A Treecreeper's call can be so high pitched that some people cannot hear it.

From Bird Watching magazine (www.birdwatching.co.uk)

Bright ideas

Toothpaste can work wonders on your tarnished and dull sterling silver. Simply rub on some toothpaste and leave for about an hour. Then wash it off and wipe dry with a towel for super-sparkly silver once more.

I wish I'd said that

"I call everyone darling, because I can't remember their names." **A great tip from actress Zsa Zsa Gabor.**

Only in Britain

Mummers' plays

Christmas Mummers' plays are a tradition dating back to the 18th century and at one time would take place in every village in England. These surviving folk dramas are short rhyming sketches that would generally include a struggle between good and evil and a comedy quack doctor.

Our Tune

On The Street Where You Live from My Fair Lady

I met Geoff in 1994. He was a lovely singer, and this was his favourite tune. We were partners for 13 years, until I lost him in 2008. Whenever I hear this song now, I picture his happy face singing with gusto and it brings a lump to my throat.

Diana Champ, Tonbridge, Kent

Photo I can't throw away

This is a photo of me, my late husband Terry and our daughters, Tina and Cindy, on our way to Terry's cousin's winter wedding in 1970 at Combe Methodist Church. I love Tina and Cindy's matching ponchos, which were kindly knitted by a friend of ours. I think we look like such a happy family group. Terry died in 2006 after 45 years of marriage, so this means a lot to me. A photo I wouldn't part with.

Judy Oliver, Stonesfield, Oxon

Recipe of the week

Oaty Apple and Cranberry Stuffing

Serves: 8-10
(makes enough to stuff an average-sized turkey)
Preparation time: 10 minutes
Cooking time: 25 minutes

◆ 1 tbsp vegetable oil
◆ 1 large onion, chopped
◆ 4 rashers smoked streaky bacon, diced
◆ 450g Bramley apples, peeled, cored and grated
◆ zest and juice of 1 lemon
◆ 1 medium egg, beaten
◆ 175g fine oatmeal
◆ 175g fresh white breadcrumbs
◆ 3 tbsp fresh sage, chopped
◆ 75g dried cranberries

1 Heat the oil in a frying pan, add the onion and bacon and fry for 5 minutes, or until pale golden. Transfer to a bowl to cool slightly.
2 Then add the rest of the ingredients, season well with a little salt and plenty of freshly ground pepper. Mix thoroughly to combine.
3 Use the stuffing to fill the neck of turkey or chicken. Roll any remaining into balls and roast in the oven alongside the bird for 20 minutes or until golden.

◆ **Top tip:** This stuffing can be made up to two days in advance and chilled until you need it resulting in less stress on the day!
© The Bramley Apple Information Service, www.bramleyapples.co.uk

My Teenage Years
My Mary Quant maxi

I did two things when I left school in 1965: I lost the puppy fat that had plagued me until then and I changed my hair from brunette to blonde highlights. Dad did not like me wearing make-up so I had not worn any until I started work, which probably saved me from a lot of skin problems. When this photo was taken, I had just mastered the art of putting on false eyelashes.

Whether going to work or out for the evening, we always dressed smartly and colourfully. I would go to the local town, usually on a Saturday morning, to buy material to make my own clothes. My one and only designer coat was a mauve Mary Quant maxi with silver flower buttons, which was very trendy. Today's clothes seem dull in comparison.

Fun was going swimming, playing table tennis or going to a local dance with friends. Our transport was usually on the back of one of the boys' motorbikes or walking.

Although I liked George Harrison of The

Linda soon mastered the art of applying false eyelashes

Beatles and thought Dave Dee, Dozy, Beaky, Mick and Tich were a lively group, none of them matched up to my favourite pop star – Billy Fury. My family went on holiday to Great Yarmouth when I was in my early teens and I talked my Dad into taking Mum, my brother Paul and me to see his show. I think my poor Dad's ears were ringing for quite a while after it was over!

Linda Hart, Romford, Essex

Bird of the week

PIC: ISTOCK

Buzzard

The Common Buzzard has become a familiar sight in recent years. The colouring varies greatly from bird to bird, leading them to be mistaken for many other birds of prey if not seen clearly. The largest example of the hawk family, it is a slow flier that's not very successful at catching moving prey. Its strategy is to sit quietly on a fence post or branch, where it's well camouflaged with its mottled brown plumage, and wait for prey to arrive.
From Bird Watching magazine (www.birdwatching.co.uk)

Bright ideas

Frozen butter pieces will make stuffing them between the skin and meat of a turkey, or chicken, a lot less messy. Why not make herb butter by mixing dried herbs into soft butter before freezing small pieces to use in the same way? Your roast meat will taste divine!

I wish I'd said that

"Some of you I consider friends, others, people I met."
The perfect way to start a speech.

Only in Britain

Bonkers Boxing Day antics

Only in Britain could you go barrel racing, play beach football or take part in a wheelbarrow race on Boxing Day! If you can drag yourself away from the television don't miss the Nippy Dipper Boxing Day Dip, in Aberdeen. From Santa suits to mermaids it has it all!

Our Tune

Yours – Vera Lynn

During the war, I shared a bedroom looking out on the town's Jockey Club, which was housing RAF personnel. We would use a torch to send messages using Morse code. So exciting, especially when I got my first date! I think of Mathew still, and often play our favourite tune.

Sylvia Archer, Tenbury Wells, Worcs

Photo I can't throw away

I was five when this photo was taken for our 1947 Christmas card. My hair was put into 'curl rags', and I was given strict instructions not to dirty my dress. The photographer placed us in position –my sister, Romayne, by my side, my brother, Alistair, looking out of the window, my mother intent on her knitting and my father absorbed in a book. I was fascinated as the photographer disappeared behind a black cloth to take the photo. **Sandy O'Neill, Yarmouth**

Recipe of the week

Mixed Berries Mulled Wine

Serves: 8-10
Preparation time: 5 minutes
Cooking time: 22 minutes

- 1 large orange
- 125g caster sugar
- 6 cloves
- 2 cinnamon sticks
- 1/4 tsp freshly grated nutmeg
- 1 vanilla pod, halved lengthways
- 2x bottles red wine
- 50ml (2 fl oz) brandy
- 200g mixed berries

1 Cut the zest of the orange in thin strips and squeeze the juice. Then place both into a large saucepan with the sugar, spices and vanilla pod.
2 Add just enough red wine to cover the ingredients and put onto a low heat, stirring continuously for 10 minutes, or until the sugar has dissolved.
3 Then turn up the heat and bring to a rapid boil for 10 minutes, or until the mixture has reduced and become slightly syrupy. Add the rest of the wine, brandy and the mixed berries and turn down the heat Gently simmer for two minutes, but do not allow to boil. Serve immediately in heatproof glasses.
© Seasonal Berries. www.seasonalberries.co.uk

My Teenage Years
Mince pie memory

Although my schooldays weren't the happiest days of my life, I did enjoy domestic science lessons (as they were known then). We were taught the fundamentals of baking biscuits, cakes and bread. I had always enjoyed helping Mum with the cooking and having the opportunity to learn new techniques was something I appreciated.

We learned how to make various types of pastry, starting with a suet pastry for a hearty steak-and-kidney pudding, progressing onto flaky pastry for vol-au-vents and ending with choux pastry for chocolate éclairs.

For Christmas we made a traditional cake and were shown how to ice it by marking out a pattern on greaseproof paper and pricking out the design on the cake surface. Mine was decorated in a lattice design and I remember the teacher showing me how to use two piping bags to get an interweaving effect. It was complicated but worthwhile when, on Christmas Day, the family admired my efforts.

Another happy memory is of my mother and me making batch after batch of mince pies in the

Joan has very fond memories of Christmas baking

week leading up to Christmas. These were given away to relatives and on Christmas Eve we made the last two batches for our own family. As I got older it became the Christmas Eve tradition to treat ourselves to a glass of sherry as a reward for our hard work. Needless to say, we were always tempted to sample an early mince pie, too, just to make sure the sherry didn't go straight to our heads!

Joan Marlow, Tamworth, Staffs

Bird of the week

Robin
PIC: ISTOCK

The cheeky Robin of the Christmas card, seen perching on a gardener's spade, is actually a feisty individual. Only the hardest of winters will see more than one Robin share a garden space. In fact, in winter an area the size of a football pitch will only be big enough for about 12 individuals, and they will aggressively see off any other Robin invading their territory. Nevertheless, their bright red breast and incredibly loud and melodious song cheer up a dull winter's day.

From Bird Watching magazine (www.birdwatching.co.uk)

Bright ideas

Hardier leftover herbs such as thyme and rosemary are robust enough to freeze as they are. Lay them flat on a baking tray and freeze, before putting into a plastic bag to store. Use in soups, roasted vegetables and meats in exactly the same way you'd use the fresh variety.

I wish I'd said that

"A clear conscience is usually the sign of a bad memory." **Anonymous**

Only in Britain

First-footing

Hogmanay, the Scottish New Year celebration, isn't complete without first-footing. This quirky tradition involves being the first person to step into a friend or neighbour's house. Traditionally, a first-footer must be male, dark, tall and handsome! And they should bring gifts of coal for warmth, cake for food and salt for wealth.

Our Tune

I'll Walk Beside You – Pat McCormick

My husband, Alf, was sent to Canada for RAF training. Unfortunately, he had an accident and was grounded. He became severely depressed. Talking one evening, I told him: "I love you dearly, and will be with you," when the voice of Pat McCormick came over the radio singing this tune.

Ida Wootton, Letchmore Heath, Watford

Photo I can't throw away

This wedding photograph is so important to my husband as he only knew one set of grandparents. He was never told by his unmarried Mother who his Father was. His Grandfather, Walter, and Grandmother, Ethel, were married on December 30, 1922. Walter died when my husband was three, so photos are the only memories he has. Knowing his maternal family is such a blessing, but what a joy it would be to have just one photograph of the paternal side.

Elle Chambers, Boston

Recipe of the week

Feed-the-masses Turkey Curry

Serves 4 (easily doubled or tripled!)
Preparation time: 10 minutes
Cooking time: 50 minutes

- 3 tbsp vegetable oil
- 1 large onion, chopped
- 1 stick celery, sliced
- 1 small red pepper
- 1 small potato, peeled and diced
- 700g Turkey breast meat, diced
- 1 tsp ground coriander
- 1 tsp ground cumin
- 1 tsp ground cinnamon
- $1/2$ tsp ground turmeric
- 1 tsp hot chilli powder
- 1 chicken stock cube
- 300ml (12 fl oz) boiling water

For the chutney:
- $1/2$ red onion, chopped
- 1 medium tomato, chopped
- 1 small bunch fresh coriander, chopped

To serve:
- Boiled white rice, warm naan bread and thick natural yogurt

1 Heat the vegetable oil in a heavy saucepan and add the onion, celery, pepper and potato. Stir to mix and cook for 4-5 minutes on a medium heat, or until everything has softened slightly.
2 Then add the turkey and stir in all the spices, cook for 5 minutes before crumbling in the stock cube and add the water. Cover, bring to the boil and simmer for 35-40 minutes.
3 Meanwhile, make the chutney by combining all the ingredients and chill. When the curry is ready, serve alongside rice, warm naan bread and dollops of yogurt and chutney.

© Change your meat not your menu, Bernard Matthews farms, www.bernardmatthewsfarms.com

Festive countdown

This homemade advent calendar makes a lovely Christmas decoration and can be used year after year.

You will need:

24 round tins with transparent lids (suitable tin favour kit available from Hobbycraft)
Christmas themed scrapbooking papers or thick wrapping paper
PVA glue
Spray adhesive
Hot glue gun
Strong card 12 inch square
1m ribbon in a colour of your choice
A selection of sequins, glitter and embellishments

1 Use the spray adhesive to stick a sheet of decorative paper to the card. To make the wreath base, use two plates to draw concentric circles and cut out.

2 Arrange your tins on to the card base and glue each base into position with the glue gun. Add the hanging ribbon and ribbon bow in the same way gluing and then leaving aside to dry.

3 Using your different patterned papers, cut 24 circles that are slightly smaller than your tin lids, so they fit inside. Then write a number (1–24) on each.

4 To finish, decorate your tin lids with your chosen embellishments and use a tiny amount of PVA glue to secure each circle to the inside of a tin lid. Leave to dry completely before filling with treats and hanging.

For more great craft projects and all your crafting supplies call 01202 596100 or visit www.hobbycraft.co.uk.

Takes 2 hours

◆ Make yours extra festive by using natural materials such as holly and mistletoe to decorate.

Quiz of the month

Can you answer the questions on these popular detective programmes? If you get stuck the answers are below.

1 In which city was The Sweeney set?

2 Name the Only Fools and Horses actor who played Jack Frost in A Touch of Frost

3 What make of car did Inspector Morse drive?

4 In Dixon of Dock Green, what was Dixon's first name?

5 What was the police station called in The Bill?

6 Z-Cars was set in which northern county?

7 This actor played the fifth doctor in Doctor Who and more importantly Campion. Can you name him?

8 Softly, Softly was the spin-off show for which police drama series?

9 Which Scottish city is Taggart set?

10 Name the Cold Feet actor who played Tommy Murphy in Murphy's Law

11 Foyle's War was set during which war?

Z–Cars was located where?

12 Can you name the actor who played Sûreté detective Commissaire Jules Maigret? Rupert Davis or Ewen Solon

13 What was Paul Temple's well known saying?

14 Which police force does Inspector Morse work for?

15 Ashes to Ashes was the sequel to which police drama series?

16 The title sequence of which cop show showed the feet of two police pounding the beat?

17 In Taggart what was Superintendent McVitie otherwise known as?

18 Name the Minder and New Tricks actor who also appeared in The Sweeney as Detective Sergeant George Carter

PIC: REXFEATURES

ANSWERS: 1) London 2) David Jason 3) Jaguar 4) George 5) Sun Hill 6) Merseyside 7) Peter Davidson 8) Z-Cars 9) Glasgow 10) James Nesbitt 11) Second World War 12) Rupert Davis 13) "by Timothy" 14) Thames Valley 15) Life on Mars 16) The Bill 17) The Biscuit 18) Dennis Waterman